green books

oekom

This book is edited
by the Heinrich Böll Foundation (www.boell.de).

ClimatePartner°
klimaneutral

Verlag | ID: 128-50040-1010-1082

This book was produced in a climate-neutral way.
Preventing, reducing and compensating for
CO_2 emissions is a fundamental principle of oekom.
The publisher compensates for unavoidable emissions
by investing in a Gold Standard project.
For more information, see www.oekom.de

Published by Green Books on behalf of oekom
www.greenbooks.co.uk

© 2016 oekom, München
oekom verlag, Gesellschaft für ökologische Kommunikation mbH
Waltherstrasse 29, 80337 München, Germany
www.oekom.de

Cover design: Andrew Corbett Design
Layout and Typeset: Reihs Satzstudio, Lohmar
Translator: Christopher Hay

Printing: CPI books GmbH, Leck

This book was printed on FSC-certified recycled paper
from controlled sources.

1. edition
All rights reserved.
Printed in Germany.
978-0-85784-415-6

Thomas Fatheuer, Lili Fuhr
and Barbara Unmüßig

INSIDE THE
GREEN
ECONOMY

PROMISES
AND PITFALLS

Contents

————

PART ONE
Why "business as usual" is not an option

PART TWO
Rampant risk:
questionable instruments and innovations

PART THREE
The Green Economy's blind spots

Preface
by Tim Jackson

———

Rethinking economics is a vital task, because our existing visions for the good life, and our economic models for achieving it, have both come badly unstuck. Financial markets are unstable. Inequality haunts even the richest societies. Resource conflicts threaten geopolitical stability and the spectre of climate change and biodiversity loss loom menacingly over our future.

Into this landscape of uncertainty steps the 'green economy': a way of thinking about economics that is supposed to take the environment into account. A promise to transform our approach both to nature and to capital. A vision to put people and planet back into the heart of economics. Green economy was the terminology adopted enthusiastically by the United Nations in advance of the Rio plus 20 Conference in 2012.

But somehow things went badly wrong. In a dubious strategy aimed at bringing high-profile financial players to the table, the UN launched its report, *Towards a Green Economy*, by claiming that 'green growth is faster than brown growth'. Scientists questioned the evidence for this claim. The G77 nations resisted it as yet another incursion of Western interests into the affairs of poorer nations. Environmental and social activists distanced themselves from its corporatist interpretations.

Even before the delegates arrived in Rio de Janeiro, the transformative promise of the green economy was dissipated in mistrust and misunderstanding. This first, extended, in-depth analysis of the concept and practices, originally published in German, seeks to elucidate the reasons for this mistrust and to re-invigorate the transformative debate, which some of the original proponents of the green economy sought to stimulate.

At the heart of this endeavour must lie a more in-depth understanding of what it means for human beings to prosper in a world of environmental and social limits. The core value proposition of the prevailing model — that more will make us happier — has signally failed to deliver — even in the affluent West.

Modern economics equates happiness with income. More is always better, in the conventional wisdom. And this comforting myth sustains the growth-based economy and motivates adherence to the status quo. The more we have in monetary terms, the better off we are deemed to be. Across the world, capitalism advances by seeking out new markets for new products: the continual throwing over of the old in favour of the new; the intrusion of the market into ever more personal areas of our lives.

In the beginning, this process can be immensely productive, leading to dramatic advances in our real standard of living. There are places where these improvements are still desperately needed. But to keep the process going in perpetuity even in the richest economies, as the system requires, we need people resolutely hooked on stuff, prepared to borrow and spend — even to mortgage their own financial future if necessary — so that they can carry on consuming.

This is where things start to fall apart. Relentless expansion leads to resource depletion. Resource depletion accelerates our impact on the planet. Chasing prosperity through material possessions can only lead us faster towards disaster. The pursuit of happiness can only lead to a profound unhappiness in the long run. Or, to cut a long story short, our idea of social progress is not just unsustainable, it is internally inconsistent.

If the vision itself were coherent, if the only route to a greater prosperity really were more material affluence, our prospect for social progress would indeed be bleak. We would find ourselves in a world in which prosperity was only ever available to the few at the expense of the many — and only to present generations at the expense of future generations. Short of railing against the malevolence of deity, we would be consigned to an unsavoury power struggle over available resources and an eventual decline into barbarism.

But, on a closer analysis, this vision of humanity as a voracious horde of self-serving novelty-seekers turns out to be, at best, incomplete and at worst wildly inaccurate. Quite often, it turns out, even economists don't really believe in it. The good news is, we don't need a radical change in human nature to achieve a lasting prosperity. The bad news is the economic model itself is still profoundly out of whack.

Originally, the Green Economy was meant to create the political space for a deeper conversation. Yet, as argued in this book, such a conversation must go beyond a shallow 'economisation' of nature and quick techno-fixes. It must resist elite attempts to protect the status quo. Rather, it must engage vigorously in the politics of power, gender, class and culture. It must establish a new 'political ecology' and engage widely in the creation of a new and more profound agenda for change. This task is as relevant today as it ever was.

June 2016

Foreword

Rio de Janeiro 2012: tens of thousands of people take to the streets in protest against what they perceive to be a misleading concept of "Green Economy". It was not the oil, coal or agribusiness corporations that had rallied the demonstrators, but social movements and NGOs, predominantly from the Global South, including a number of the Heinrich Böll Foundation's partner organisations. The occasion was the United Nations Conference on Sustainable Development (Rio+20), an event that, 20 years after the 1992 Earth Summit, was set to establish "Green Economy" as a new global paradigm. These protests against the vision of a Green Economy provoked a divided response. Shouldn't we be directing all our efforts towards overcoming the "brown", fossil-fuel economy? Isn't Green Economy exactly what the environmental movement has been demanding for decades? Indeed. But the critical question is what it means, and how the concept of a Green Economy is spelt out in reality. Not everything that sails under a green flag is worthy of the name.

The criticism of truncated and misleading notions of the Green Economy does not dismiss the hope of a sustainable future and a "greening" of the economy; rather, it addresses those concepts defined by key players like the World Bank, the OECD and business-based think tanks, which currently frame most people's understanding of Green Economy.

Whether we like it or not, it is a contentious issue. Yet for all the disputes, the discourse does take up the pivotal question confronting us today: faced with so many crises requiring urgent attention, can we accomplish a fundamental transformation of the economy and society towards sustainability?

Along with democracy and human rights, this is the major topic on the Heinrich Böll Foundation's agenda. We facilitate this transformation in diverse ways — with workable scenarios for a successful energy transition, for agricultural policy reform, for alternative mobility and for sustainable urban development. We do not shy away from dialogue with the industry. We devote the majority of our resources to critically appraising the fossil-fuel economy and agroindustry. At the same time, we support many stakeholders worldwide who are striving for different modes of production and lifestyles and are trying out new ideas of social coexistence. Advancing the necessary "major transformation" requires both approaches: visionary alternatives and incremental changes.

We see ourselves as a catalysing force as well as a think tank, and that means engaging with the various strategies and discourses that aim to contribute to social and environmental transformation. A departure from "business as usual" has been politically tenable for some time. But the question of how the transformation is to be effected is a matter of dispute. How is this transformation defined? Which tools and mechanisms are required? What promises does it make? It will come as no surprise to anyone that such questions arouse controversy.

Even within the Heinrich Böll Foundation, the various concepts of a sustainable, environmentally friendly and participatory economy are the subject of intense debate. The spectrum ranges from blueprints for a green industrial revolution to the critique of mainstream concepts of a Green Economy that claim to accomplish the transformation purely by means of technological innovation and more market influence, holding out the promise that all will be well. But is the expansion of market mechanisms really appropriate for halting climate change and environmental degradation? How much and which type of political regulation is needed to promote the kind of structural change that will be necessary to move towards a sustainable and just economy? These are just some of the questions explored in this volume.

Although it is correct that "prices should tell the environmental truth", we are critical of the general financialisation of nature (and of society). Likewise, the relationship between innovation and limitation, efficiency and sufficiency requires critical examination. Ultimately, it is about the key role of politics in the process of environmental transformation.

This book is therefore devoted primarily to a critical assessment of mainstream concepts of a Green Economy. The authors shed light on aspects that tend to go unnoticed in this context — questions of human rights, participation and democracy, for instance. In addition, they discuss the role of politics in a world in which all challenges are increasingly defined in terms of economic imperatives.

To that extent, this publication itself is part of the controversy. The views expressed by the authors are their own. Within the Foundation we discuss ways out of the environmental and social crisis with great passion. In doing so, we articulate diverse views and ideas about which instruments, what balance of market and state, how much growth and which innovations and alliances will move us forward. This book sets out to generate creative tension. Quite intentionally, it does not set forth any major counterproposal to the conventional definition of Green Economy. Rather, our aim is to encourage a process of reappraisal and reflection. In that spirit, we look forward to engaging in the debate on a just and sustainable future within our global partner network.

Every campaign needs champions. While thinking about, discussing and writing this book, the authors have greatly benefited from others' advice, ideas and encouragement. We would particularly like to thank Christine Chemnitz, Ulrich Hoffmann, Heike Löschmann, Ulrich Brand, Jutta Kill and Wolfgang Sachs for their time and dedication in commenting on the manuscript. We also wish to express our gratitude to Bernd Rheinberg for his professional advice and his great patience.

Barbara Unmüßig and Ralf Fücks
Presidents of the Heinrich Böll Foundation

Berlin, June 2016

Introduction

The Green Economy is a source of both hope and controversy. For some, it shows the way out of permanent environmental and economic crises and promises to reconcile ecology and economics — a long cherished Utopia. It fosters the hope that we can hang on to our current high standard of material prosperity. For those who have so far been excluded from prosperity, inclusion is supposed to become possible thanks to the Green Economy paradigm. And both goals are to be accomplished while keeping within the biophysical boundaries of our planet. For others, Green Economy is "business as usual" dressed up in green, or merely a green-washing manoeuvre that does not stop the overexploitation of the planet and even exacerbates social disparities.

The Green Economy has become a matter of contention. It is *the* environmental policy topic, prompting heated discussion between North and South, East and West, grassroots movements and big politics, upper classes and underclasses. The debate surrounding Green Economy causes frayed tempers because it is about so much more than environmental conservation: how do we want to live in the future? How do we want to share our planet's limited resources with each other? What is the "good life"?

The attempt to establish the Green Economy as the new paradigm reached its climax in the preparations for and events around the Rio +20 conference in the year 2012. The conference failed as an endeavour, but did manage to convey the distinctive feature of this paradigm into global climate and environmental policy: the economy itself should lead the way out of environmental crises — including the way out of the political blind alleys of multilateral negotiations on climate change mitigation and ecosystem conservation. In practice the impact of this paradigm became evident in 2015 at COP 21 in Paris: A process meant to deliver a global, comprehensive, legally binding and equitable climate regime has turned into a flower-basket of voluntary national commitments with hardly any verification or comparability — let alone accountability. The anchoring of an ambitious aim to "pursue efforts to limit temperature increase to 1.5 °C above pre-industrial levels" (Paris Agreement, Article 2, para. 1 [a]) is, admittedly, widely celebrated as a major achievement, and the contribution of civil society pressure to get there was well acknowledged. The explicit reference to this temperature goal is a significant improvement over what was achievable in Copenhagen 2009 and deserves to be celebrated. It can now be held against anyone daring to suggest opening a new coal mine anywhere on the planet. In that sense, many observers viewed the Paris outcome according to the market signal it gives to investors.[1]

However, if one dares to step back a little from the day to day business of climate policy making, there is no way around acknowledging that we have utterly failed because we have become too comfortable with a very narrow vision of the problem itself. As Wolfgang Sachs puts it: "A history of environmental policy as the history of forgotten alternatives has not yet been written."[2] We have taken many wrong turns along the way: first by accepting that climate policy was about reducing emissions alone (thus tackling only the output side), then believing that a tonne of CO_2 not only equals any other tonne of CO_2 no matter where it was emitted but that other greenhouse gases can be counted in CO_2-equivalents. And finally by buying into flexible mechanisms of emissions trading and offsetting.

This carbon-centric worldview is an essential part of the Green Economy debate — the two can hardly be held apart. The world is currently on the verge of taking yet another wrong turn by embracing the idea of "negative emissions," with the goal of reaching "net zero emissions." This shift implies that the world can continue to produce emissions so long as new technologies are invented to suck carbon out of the atmosphere at a later stage — instead of embarking on a radical trajectory that leaves fossil fuels in the ground, changes our agricultural systems and restores our natural ecosystems. But this idea is actually more of a myth — we can't continue to emit massive amounts of CO_2 and even establish new coal-burning power plants while claiming to address climate change through new technologies.

The obsession with carbon metrics helps to promote nuclear energy, natural gas extraction (including fracking), biofuels and other risky and harmful technologies, as long as they can claim to produce less carbon-emission than was expected without them. None of this will bring us any closer to the transformational changes in self and society that are required to deal with climate change and depend on the preservation and utilisation of diverse ideas and approaches that believe in non-linear change. In the monoculture of carbon metrics, real alternatives become literally unthinkable.

The Green Economy as an exit from "business as usual"-thinking based on linear change sounds good because the diagnosis that we cannot carry on producing and consuming as we used to seems to be shared by ever-growing sections of the economic and political elites. It is "concern" about dwindling production factors and the scarcity of key resources (oil, land, water, biodiversity and mineral resources) that drives technological innovations forward. The physical limits of the planet threaten the capitalist growth model.

So the departure from "business as usual" has indeed become politically tenable. But is there really political and social consensus about what this means? Is the departure from "business as usual" really happening? Is "business as usual" not still the default option, while the exit from fossil-fuelled and resource-intensive economics is the niche option at best? What policies do we have for overcoming social disparity and socio-ecological injustice within and between societies, particularly given the context of climate change and resource scarcity?

Our view of the realities is influenced by whatever science provides for us in the way of knowledge and data. In the first part of the book we demonstrate what a huge task changing course really is.

Never before in human history has there been so much systematised and concentrated knowledge as in the context of global environmental crises. Nowadays we are confronted daily, at least via the media, with the realities of social inequality, poverty, refugee flows and wars. We know all about the present and future dangers of catastrophic global climate change and we can be live spectators of species extinction.

If in this book we show the terrifying picture of "business as usual" and refer once again to the scientific data on planetary boundaries, we do so because we want to point out the scale and urgency of the political and social task of changing course. The Green Economy — as the majority of its advocates in the economy, politics and some supranational institutions understands it — correctly identifies many problems but downplays the magnitude of the necessary reorientation.

Admittedly, our discourse- and power-critical analyses of the conceptual assumptions underlying the Green Economy and its practice, particularly in climate change mitigation and nature conservation, but also in agriculture, paint an alarming picture of the present and the future. Nevertheless, we see the analyses of the planetary boundaries and social inequality and injustice as the starting point for a positive vision that does not induce paralysis but rather incites radical action: they clarify the challenge we face if we want to move closer towards the Utopia of a good life for all people on Earth, a democratic, more equitable and peaceful world within the planetary boundaries.

The permanent social, economic and environmental crises are closely interlinked. Discovering how environmentally sustainable innovations can be generally integrated with normative principles of justice, democratic control and participation, and with universal human rights, must be part of the journey towards a fundamental transformation of our economy and society. Acknowledging the size of the task is the stimulus for this process, which many have already started in order to find the social and technical innovations that we need.

Many Green Economy advocates also see how great the challenges are. But when it comes to solutions, all too often, they confine themselves to technological innovations and new markets. Such a strategy truncates the challenge to the economic level and creates the impression that a quick fix is possible without any major disruptions.

Indeed, it is all about hope. Resignation is no source of good counsel. Breaking people down into optimists and pessimists, which is unfortunately a common tactic in environmental debates, is too simplistic in our view. Radical realism is the core of our understanding of a political ecology that needs to gain social majorities and does not shy away from unpleasant tasks. Even if that is difficult: technological and social innovations must be much more closely interwoven; as broad a social and participatory search as possible and corresponding alliances are needed.

The great task will be to continue the project of modernity, embracing the latest knowledge about planetary boundaries as well as the old vision of broad democratic participation and an end to poverty and injustice. This is no small undertaking; it is political and ethical, and it calls for passion and tenacity. It will not lead to a new Garden of Eden. It will be embattled with social and environmental struggles.

The Green Economy — as it is currently conceived and practised in the economic mainstream — does not face up to this Utopia. It offers more instant answers, which are mainly economic and technological. At the heart of the Green Economy is an appealing promise: we can change course, and then all will be well. More technological innovation will enable us to bring about the efficiency revolution and to decouple economic output from energy and material consumption. Not that these are in way unnecessary! Without new ideas and inventions we are marching on the spot, and will never master the complex challenges of the future. But they alone are not enough. The task is much greater.

In all proposals for green transformation, innovation has keystone status. In this book we demonstrate, with reference to many examples, where innovative pathways are bringing forth new "green sins", and particularly where innovation is leading down blind alleys. We likewise describe how innovation has to be socially and environmentally embedded in order to make genuinely sustainable contributions to social and environmental transformation, and explore whether or not the decoupling of a country's economic output (GDP) from the consumption of nature and materials is illusory.

All the Green Economy conceptions, which we discuss mainly in the second part of the book, make the economy pivotal to their proposals on sustainability. What is more, they proclaim economics to be the overall system and ecology a subsystem, instead of the reverse. This Green Economy redefines nature, not the economy. (We are aware of parallels to other economification tendencies, e.g. affecting care work or development co-operation, but these are not explicit topics of this book.) And the homo oeconomicus is once more at the centre of all solutions.

"It's the economy, stupid!" Of course it will not work without the economy—and the same applies to the idea of a comprehensive ecological and social transformation. In the theory and practice of Green Economy, however, there is an ominous paradox: it wishes to tackle the obvious failure of previous economics by using the old tools in new fields, namely realising the public and private values (valorisation) of nature and other domains of life. The assumption is straightforward: we need a Green Economy so that market failure—as is universally attested with respect to climate change and biodiversity—can finally be overcome. Instead of more political intervention and regulation, more market is held to be the answer to these two environmental crises, with new market-based instruments aimed at finally calling a halt to the exclusion of nature and certain ecosystem services from the capitalist market.

At the end of the book we deal with the blind spots in the various Green Economy conceptions. One of the Green Economy's very major blind spots is its failure to acknowledge social actors, blanking out the social and human rights impacts of some economic practices and ignoring social reproduction (the "care economy") as part of that economy, as do all traditional concepts of the economy. Green Economy is blind to power and politics and to questions of justice and democracy.

We have chosen to deliver an extensive critique of the Green Economy—as transmitted to us conceptually and experienced in practice

so far—because under the banner of an intrinsically positive concept, it suggests that the world as we know it can largely be preserved
with a more efficient and resource-saving new, but green, growth paradigm. The Green Economy acts as if growth-fixated technological
innovation were the only possible answer, and the important question of how we can create a better future using *fewer* resources *differently* and *diversely* is deemed obsolete.

While we criticise the Green Economy as we know it to date, we do
not want to scrap the notion of an economy that recognises of planetary boundaries and normative foundations such as universal as well
as economic, social and cultural human rights. That is not exactly
how many the Green Economy concepts have been developed, however. They have emerged from institutions that have independently
and wilfully put concepts on the table that have never been subjected
to broader societal or parliamentary debate.

Criticising the Green Economy is not without its risks. Are there
not more pressing topics? Should we not concentrate our publications and political energy on the battle against the brown fossil-fuel
economy? Are we too harsh on those who have recognised the problems and are looking for quick and pragmatic answers, for which
political majorities could be garnered here and now?

Moreover, the world is being torn apart by wars and terror; millions of refugees are on the move. Do we not risk making overwhelming demands when we seek to come to grips not only with the planet's huge environmental crises but also with the dispute over right and
wrong solutions?

Focusing attention on all the structural causes of the many crises
and working on solutions really does verge on an overwhelming demand. Since the causes are all interdependent in one way or another,
however, in place of sectorial action, integrated and transdisciplinary
perspectives must be practised in the search for answers as to how
a social and ecological transformation can be accomplished. Green
Economy can and will reconfigure our economy in the context of environmentally and socially sustainable innovation in such ways that
we will consume somewhat fewer resources, pollute the environment

somewhat less and it will offer better, more future-proofed jobs. The environmental trend reversal will have to be more radical, though. Equally, the justice and redistribution policies with which poverty and hunger can be halted will need to be embedded in the planetary boundaries and in democratic processes.

In the policy-making arena, the governments of the world continue to indulge in irresponsibility. On the multilateral level, the steps taken are far smaller than would seriously be needed to halt the immense destruction of nature. The new global Sustainable Development Goals (SDGs), the new socio-environmental guardrails of the United Nations (UN), will do little to change this because, as they stand, they are entirely non-binding and not particularly ambitious. The acceptance of the Paris Agreement at the COP 21 climate change conference in December 2015 is a diplomatic breakthrough. Yet it hardly responded to the enormity of the challenge and the needs and pressure from people on the ground demanding a global deal anchored in climate justice.

In this book we describe the major negative trends of Green Economy because they counteract the many positive approaches like the success of renewable energies. At the same time, we refrain from describing concrete alternatives in practice because they have already been described — in this and other contexts — prolifically elsewhere. We are interested in the possibilities of a change in course in political practice, and therefore we analyse which theoretical assumptions and which actors are really behind the new Green Economy narrative. In that sense our approach is discourse-critical and power-critical. It calls for answers as to how society can be liberated somewhat from the dominance of economics, or how the "embedding of the market" (Karl Polanyi) into society can be brought back to fruition.

This book is an invitation to join the debate. We are neither the arbiters of truth, nor do we claim to have perfect insight into the crises and solutions with all their diversity, complexity and interdependency. Indeed, it is doubtful that any individual alive can make such a claim. But for that very reason, our concern is to put forward a fundamental and maximally comprehensive critique of Green Economy conceptions. That critique questions the basic assumptions and hypotheses and investigates the implications of the solutions proffered by such conceptions—and hence, offers a foundation for a differentiated, well-grounded and constructive debate and sets signposts for those seeking and struggling to chart viable pathways for the future.

PART ONE

Why "business as usual" is not an option

1

The dominance
of the climate killers

"The planet's future is in jeopardy." Hardly anyone seriously contradicts this statement. Our insight into global interdependencies has advanced hugely in recent decades and brought us to this unanimous conviction. It is no longer just a wake-up call from ecologists, but a scientifically founded statement that is based on countless individual studies.

One of the milestones in the systematic documentation and classification of environmental crises, for example, is the United Nations Millennium Ecosystem Assessment (MA) initiated in the year 2001, which describes the condition and the loss of ecosystems and biodiversity. It was the predicament of climate change, however, which prompted the strongest effort. Never before in human history has there been such a comprehensive attempt to systematise and concentrate knowledge, and to articulate politically relevant conclusions, as in the context of climate change.

Founded as early as 1988, also under the aegis of the United Nations, the Intergovernmental Panel on Climate Change (IPCC) is a unique undertaking to achieve a global, scientifically founded consensus. And, in fact, the insight that humankind is heading for catastrophic, self-inflicted climate change has almost become a kind of global common sense. Admittedly, there is a camp of sceptics and deniers, but scientifically (if not politically, in all places) that camp remains insignificant.

Planetary boundaries

The "planetary boundaries" approach of the Stockholm Resilience Center coordinated by Johan Rockström has become an important frame of reference for the systematisation of global environmental crises.[3] This approach attempts to identify global processes that threaten the equilibrium of the Earth (as a system). The researchers around Rockström are conscious that global trends are caused by a multiplicity of local processes. Fundamental to the approach is the assumption of local and global thresholds, the crossing of which has unforeseeable consequences. It is clear, of course, that thresholds or boundaries cannot be fixed with total precision. The very fact that there are "tipping points" in many ecosystems creates uncertainty for precise predictions. The planetary boundaries approach, however, is less about detailed predictions than about defining a safe framework within which the pressures are controllable, as far as we can humanly tell based on the knowledge currently available. The approach attempts to incorporate important trends even if they are not all located on the same level: human activities consume non-renewable resources and destroy nature; at the same time they make demands on the capacities of the oceans, the land and the atmosphere—so-called sinks—which absorb pollutants. Despite a certain amount of (well-founded and important) conceptual criticism,[4] the planetary boundaries approach is largely accepted. UN organisations and the European Commission now make reference to it.

Unsurprisingly, biodiversity loss and advancing climate change number among the most important threats to the "safe operating space" that is identified by the planetary boundaries approach. Far less prominent in general awareness is the third way, in which we significantly overstep our planetary boundaries: nitrogen loading of soils and waters. The planetary boundaries approach calls heightened attention to the fact that the global challenges are multidimensional and interconnected. Finally, the federal-government appointed German Advisory Council on Global Change (WBGU) issued a flagship report entitled "World in Transition — A Social Contract for Sustainability", which describes the global environmental problems existing today as "dramatic" and urges a major transformation. This ultimately casts doubt on modernity and calls for economic, political, social and cultural changes on a scale that would affect all industrialised and newly industrialising countries. One of the WBGU's conclusions is this: "The 'fossil-nuclear metabolism' of industrial society has no future. The longer we cling to it, the higher the price will be for future generations. However, there are alternatives which would at least give all people access to the chance of a good life within the boundaries of the natural environment. Without a global agreement to actually dare to experiment with these alternatives, we will not manage to find our way out of the crisis of late modernity."[5]

So the departure from "business as usual" (BAU) has become politically tenable. The phrase "BAU is not an option" has certainly become the frame of reference for certain studies and certain strategic approaches, by the World Bank or the OECD,[6] for example. What is more, the economic risk of climate change — i.e. the loss of important natural production factors like water, land, mineral and biotic resources and biodiversity — is at the centre of a rethink by some industry actors. In that light, a stepwise decarbonisation of the global economy and the preservation of such resources seem possible, at least.

But is a departure from BAU really taking place? Is the right course being set for this, politically? Is it not the case that BAU is still the default option, and decarbonisation the niche? Is what is being offered to us as a way out of multiple crises actually nothing but BAU — and thus the option most beneficial for precisely those parties which would have the most to lose in the event of a departure from the current economic and developmental paradigm?

The world's fossil economy

In 2014, the latest findings regarding the threat to our planet's life support base were summarised by the IPCC's Fifth Assessment Report of the state of knowledge on climate change. At the same time the "New Climate Economy" report updated the 2006 Stern Review in respect of the economic consequences and options for action in times of climate change.

Two unsettling findings with reference to climate change were brought out clearly in both reports: human-induced emissions of greenhouse gases rose more steeply than ever before in the years from 2000 to 2010 — that is to say, in a period in which climate change had long been a known danger, the UN Framework Convention on Climate Change had created a multilateral negotiation framework, and numerous initiatives had already been implemented worldwide to combat climate change, not least Germany's nationwide process of energy system transformation known as the "energy transition" *(Energiewende)*.

The current figures clearly show that the bulk of emissions and emissions growth is caused by the burning of fossil fuels. If we seriously wish to combat climate change, then we must talk primarily about coal, oil and gas.

The rising emissions from fossil fuels combine with another globally observable tendency, and together, they form a highly explosive mix: through the exploitation of ever-new oil and gas deposits (in the deep sea, for instance), through the exploration of tar sands and the use of fracking technology, oil and gas remain highly accessible, not to mention the immense reserves of coal. The extraction of these "unconventional" natural gas and petroleum reserves results in considerably more emissions than from conventional sources. This is mainly due to the water- and energy-intensive production methods used. The production of petroleum from tar sands, for example, generates three to five times the greenhouse gas emissions of conventional petroleum production.[7]

Coal – the climate killer

Coal contributes more to global greenhouse gas emissions than any other energy source. In 2014 it was responsible for emitting 14.2 gigatonnes of CO_2. That is 44 per cent of all energy-related carbon dioxide emissions, and more than one-quarter of all greenhouse gas emissions. The German Federal Institute for Geosciences and Natural Resources (BGR) estimates the world's coal reserves at 968 gigatonnes (= 968 billion tonnes). To have a 50 per cent chance of keeping under this limit, the CO_2 content of the atmosphere must be kept under 450 parts per million. That means that humanity must emit no more than 1,000 gigatonnes of CO_2 by 2050. That is possible only if 88 per cent of the currently confirmed coal reserves stay in the ground, along with one-third of the mineral oil and half the natural gas reserves. Our consumption of coal will have to fall sharply, from 1.07 tonnes per person today to only 80 kilograms in 2050.

Take Germany, for example: In 2014, more than one-quarter of the electricity produced came from lignite, and its output of 178 million tonnes a year makes Germany the world's biggest producer. The industry has benefited from 95 billion euros in subsidies (in real terms) since 1970, and open-cast mines have gobbled up 176,000 hectares of land. Current mines cover 60,000 hectares. Over a 90-year period, more than 230 villages and towns with almost 110,000 inhabitants have had to make way for lignite mining in Germany. Vast open pit mines exist in other countries as well. The largest is located in the US and covers 260 square kilometres. Mining's destructive exploitation of nature and long-term impacts, not least on the hydrological cycle, are immense — but the issue of who pays these costs in the long run is still unresolved. ▪

Source: COAL ATLAS – Facts and figures on a fossil fuel[8]

Leakages also play a major role. Large quantities of methane are emitted into the atmosphere from shale gas development. According to Robert Howarth from Cornell University this amounts to an estimated 12 per cent of total production considered over the full life cycle. Methane is a very powerful greenhouse gas that is over 100-fold more effective in absorbing heat than carbon dioxide (86-fold when averaged over a 20-year period following emission). The overall climate effect of shale gas can be almost double that of coal.[9] If humankind burns just the currently available oil and gas deposits, then a 2 °C warming limit (let alone 1.5 °C) is no longer achievable.[10]

For the most part, the maximum extraction rate for easily accessible, conventional petroleum ("peak oil") has already been reached or exceeded. The exploitation of new, more inaccessible and more emissions-intensive sources of petroleum and natural gas is associated with immense financial costs, high energy inputs, and both social and environmental impacts.

Our problem is not at all that petroleum will shortly run out, and certainly not any lack of coal — we still have more than enough with which to destroy our planet, our climate and our life support base. The currently low oil price has given us a breathing space by slowing down some of the new high-risk and high-cost investments. We need to ensure that we use it well to redirect investment into renewable energies and related infrastructure.

In the year 2009 the journal *Nature* published a groundbreaking study which calculated, for the first time, something like a global CO_2 budget. The outcome was that if the calculated budget is not adhered to, the maximum tolerable level of warming, i.e. an average of 2 °C above the preindustrial level, cannot be achieved. In other words, if we maintain our current pace, we can only continue to burn our customary amounts of carbon, petroleum and natural gas for approximately 13 more years — and then our globally justifiable CO_2 budget will have been exhausted. The remainder is "unburnable carbon" — a concept that was coined by the Carbon Tracker Initiative (CTI) and has become an important benchmark in global climate policy. The Initiative calculated that 2795 gigatonnes of CO_2 are in the confirmed oil, gas and carbon reserves held in private and state ownership and traded on the global exchanges. CTI contrasts this figure to a global tolerable maximum carbon budget of 565 gigatonnes. So the upshot is that four-fifths of reserves are unburnable carbon.[11]

What these calculations mean in concrete terms for the use of individual fossil resources (including their geographical distribution) was calculated by two scientists at University College London (UCL) and published in early 2015 in the journal *Nature*:[12] according to them, we may only burn around 10 per cent of the currently known global coal reserves, two-thirds of the petroleum and approximately 50 per cent of the natural gas reserves if we are serious about keeping to a 2 °C limit.

In an article in *Rolling Stone* magazine, Bill McKibben, founder of the organisation 350.org, affirmed the Carbon Tracker Initiative's calculations as the foundation for a broad and global divestment movement: he urged universities, municipalities, cities, investors and many others to withdraw their investments from fossil fuels.[13] What 350.org and the climate movement see as a moral necessity, and as something capable of withdrawing the fossil-fuel industry's "social licence", i.e. its reputation, thus becomes a riskmanagement issue for institutional investors, pension funds and governments. On the assumption that politics in the foreseeable future will take effective steps against climate change and will ultimately restrict the consumption of fossil fuels, many of today's investments will become stranded assets, and a new financial crisis based on a "carbon bubble" might even threaten global markets, because carbon could rapidly turn into a new speculation bubble. It is good that some institutional and state investors (such as the Norwegian pension fund or the insurance company Allianz) are already withdrawing from some (mostly coal) carbon projects in order to make their institutions future-proof. But as yet, the risk of a financial market bubble is far from averted. Fossil-fuel corporations and their investors are effectively placing bets that our governments will not be capable of introducing sufficiently ambitious climate policies in time.

The fossil-fuel lobby

The Intergovernmental Panel on Climate Change and increasingly also the International Energy Agency acknowledge that two-thirds to four-fifths of the fossil reserves must be left in the ground if we want to stay below the 2 °C threshold.[14] Thanks to the available scientific findings, particularly from the IPCC, policy-makers are aware that they have to set the right course for an exit from fossil energy and create appropriate framework conditions. At the moment, however, politics is not acting to reconfigure the fossil energy matrix in the manner that is necessary. Yet the rapid transition to a new energy system based on renewable energies would be possible, both technically and economically. The fact that it is not happening is largely due to the global fossil-fuel lobby's immense influence on policy. Industrialisation on the basis of fossil fuels has created a position of economic predominance for companies in that category (and a few trade unions), which these convert into direct political influence. Moreover, the bulk of fossil-fuel reserves is in state ownership and is mined, traded and consumed by state-owned companies. In such cases it is almost impossible to separate industrial from political interests. The added complication of weak governance structures and rampant corruption — as is the case in many resource-rich developing countries — amplifies the tendency to safeguard clientele interests and hence revenues from the commercialisation of fossil resources.

Regarding the question of who takes responsibility for climate change, in recent years astonishing findings have come to light: just 90 producers of coal, petroleum, natural gas and cement, known as the "carbon majors" — private, public and state-owned corporations as well as government-run industries[15] — have been responsible for 65 per cent of emissions since the beginning of industrialisation.[16] The world's 35 largest coal producers were alone responsible for one-third of global emissions between 1988 and 2013. These corporations have generated billions in profits. Although the harmfulness of CO_2 emissions had been recognised at the latest by 1988, when the Intergovernmental Panel on Climate Change was founded, these companies have not been held accountable — either financially or legally — for the harm that was done and continues to result from their products. Some recent developments give hope that this era of impunity might come to an end: The New York attorney general has begun an investigation of Exxon Mobil to determine whether the company lied to the public about the risks of climate change or to investors about how such risks may affect their investments. And the National Human Rights Commission in the Philippines is pursuing an investigation into the human rights abuses caused by the carbon majors in the context of climate change and ocean acidification. The carbon majors study puts the question about responsibility for climate change on a robust footing, making it possible for the first time to apportion responsibility to individual corporations, backed by figures.[17]

But instead of taking the analyses of advancing global warming and the necessary restructuring of the fossil-nuclear energy supply seriously, our governments continue to rely on greater exploitation of fossil resources globally, and even to subsidise this. According to a 2014 study by Oilchange International and the Overseas Development Institute, the G20 governments are spending an annual 88 billion US dollars on public subsidies for the exploration of new fossil reserves,[18] although it is already clear that at least 80 per cent of what we have already found must not be burnt.

The companies making up the carbon majors are often backed by very powerful private individuals. A good example are the brothers Charles and David Koch — two of the richest men on our planet — who control a business empire with major interests in the oil and gas industry. With their net wealth, which they have increased since 2005 from ten to over 100 billion US dollars, they can influence American politics as they see fit. Thus, in past years, they have impeded not only climate legislation but also progressive policies in the spheres of health, workers' rights, immigration and equality.[19]

Overview: the Carbon Majors

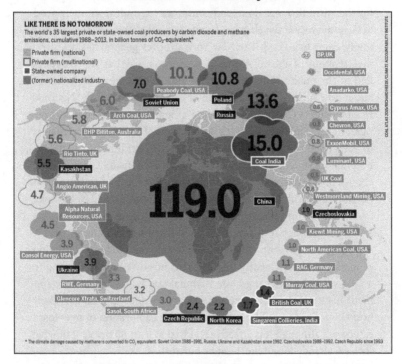

LIKE THERE IS NO TOMORROW
The world's 35 largest private or state-owned coal producers by carbon dioxide and methane emissions, cumulative 1988–2013, in billion tonnes of CO_2-equivalent*

- Private firm (national)
- Private firm (multinational)
- State-owned company
- (former) nationalized industry

10.1 — Peabody Coal, USA
10.8 — Poland
7.0 — Soviet Union
6.0 — Arch Coal, USA
13.6 — Russia
5.8 — BHP Billiton, Australia
5.6 — Rio Tinto, UK
5.5 — Kasakhstan
15.0 — Coal India
4.7 — Anglo American, UK
119.0 — China
4.5 — Alpha Natural Resources, USA
3.9 — Consol Energy, USA
3.9 — Ukraine
3.3 — RWE, Germany
3.2 — Glencore Xtrata, Switzerland
3.0 — Sasol, South Africa
2.4 — Czech Republic
2.2 — North Korea
1.7 — Singareni Collieries, India

0.2 — BP, UK
0.3 — Occidental, USA
0.4 — Anadarko, USA
0.5 — Cyprus Amax, USA
0.5 — Chevron, USA
0.5 — ExxonMobil, USA
0.5 — Luminant, USA
0.5 — UK Coal
0.8 — Westmoreland Mining, USA
1.0 — Czechoslovakia
1.0 — Kiewit Mining, USA
1.0 — North American Coal, USA
1.1 — RAG, Germany
1.1 — Murray Coal, USA
1.4 — British Coal, UK

COAL ATLAS 2015/RICHARD HEEDE/CLIMATE ACCOUNTABILITY INSTITUTE

* The climate damage caused by methane is converted to CO_2 equivalent. Soviet Union 1988–1991, Russia, Ukraine and Kazakhstan since 1992. Czechoslovakia 1988–1992, Czech Republic since 1993

Chevron, ExxonMobil, Saudi Aramco, BP, Gazprom, Shell and the German companies RWE and RAG Steinkohle are global players in the carbon market. The chart above is based on data which Richard Heede from the Climate Accountability Institute compiled exclusively for the Coal Atlas, published by the Heinrich Böll Foundation and Friends of the Earth International. The data come from his research on carbon majors[20]—the world's largest fossil-fuel producers—for the Climate Justice Programme. The chart only lists coal producers (private, state-owned and nationalised). Some of the companies also produce(d) oil and gas, in which case only their (former) coal business was analysed. Only data from 1988 onwards—the year in which the IPCC was established and the Toronto Climate Conference called for initial reduction targets—were incorporated into the above chart, whereas Richard Heede's data go back as far as 1750.

Source: COAL ATLAS – Facts and figures on a fossil fuel[21]

Renewable energies are gaining ground
but fossil-fuel expansion dominates

Despite the immense power of the carbon lobby, there are signs of a small global energy transition: not only in Europe but worldwide, renewable energies are gaining ground. In part this is why 2014 was the first year, according to International Energy Agency statistics, in which the global emissions from energy production did not rise but stagnated at the 2013 level, although the global economy grew by three per cent. The reason, in the Agency's view, is that economic growth (GDP) is starting to decouple from fossil fuel consumption.[22]

Even though the production of renewable energies is growing rapidly, globally it is not yet sufficient to replace fossil sources. Despite huge growth rates, at the moment renewable energies cannot cover even ten per cent of global energy demand, even taking the controversial hydroelectric power into account. Furthermore, with the installation of wind turbines, solar modules and the development of storage technologies, demand is rising for mineral and metal resources (for example lithium, rare earths, cobalt), leading in turn to social and environmental crises in the resource-rich countries (especially in Africa, Asia and Latin America). Renewable energies are not intangible.

Conversion to renewable energy sources will not automatically involve decentralisation or a loss of power on the part of the old energy giants, for the large oil corporations are also investing in wind parks and biofuels. Even the large mining corporations recognise the signs of the times and are backing renewable energies — with considerable negative social and environmental consequences, in the case of big dams. A lower-emission energy mix does not, by itself, herald an end to the exploitation of people and nature.

Today, growth in global energy production is happening predominantly in countries outside the OECD, with China taking a commanding lead. This is linked with a trend towards deindustrialisation in the USA and Europe. In the classic industrialised nations, industrial production is falling as a share of economic output because of

New hope, made in China

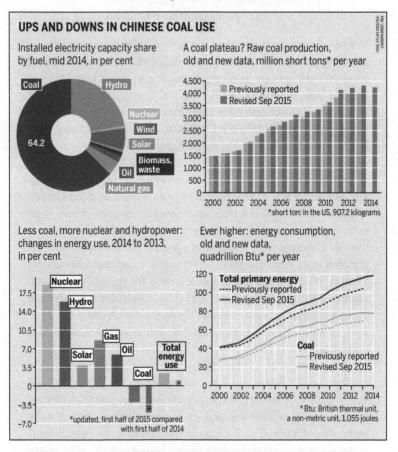

UPS AND DOWNS IN CHINESE COAL USE

Installed electricity capacity share by fuel, mid 2014, in per cent

Coal 64.2 | Hydro | Nuclear | Wind | Solar | Biomass, waste | Oil | Natural gas

A coal plateau? Raw coal production, old and new data, million short tons* per year

Previously reported
Revised Sep 2015

*short ton: in the US, 907.2 kilograms

Less coal, more nuclear and hydropower: changes in energy use, 2014 to 2013, in per cent

Nuclear | Hydro | Solar | Gas | Oil | Coal | Total energy use

*updated, first half of 2015 compared with first half of 2014

Ever higher: energy consumption, old and new data, quadrillion Btu* per year

Total primary energy
---- Previously reported
— Revised Sep 2015

Coal
---- Previously reported
— Revised Sep 2015

*Btu: British thermal unit, a non-metric unit, 1,055 joules

COAL ATLAS 2015/EIA, CARBON BRIEF, NEA

2014 was different. For the first time in over three decades, China burned less coal than in the previous year. Consumption declined by 2.9 per cent, and imports slumped by around 11 per cent. Not long ago, the International Energy Agency predicted that both figures would continue to rise until 2020. Despite the decline in coal, power consumption was up by 3.9 per cent, and gross domestic product rose by more than 7 per cent. It is unclear whether this decoupling is a blip or a turning point. It is likely to be related to an increase in the use of other fuels.

Source: COAL ATLAS – Facts and figures on a fossil fuel[23]

the partial offshoring of production to China. This makes climate targets easier to achieve in Europe, of course — some of the emission sources have simply been exported to China.

The example of China is illustrative: while the country has invested massively and successfully in the expansion of wind and solar energy, this is not changing the energy matrix fundamentally, or is only doing so very slowly. Fossil fuels and renewable energies are growing in parallel globally. In addition, many governments around the world still bank on using or even expanding nuclear power. Even so, renewable energies have outgrown their niche, and new installations, these days, are dominated by wind and solar power. Since 2007, for example, these account for more additional capacity in the EU than all other forms of energy. They were last reported to have risen to a 79 per cent share of newly installed power plant capacity; in other words, four out of five new power plants are run on renewable technology.[24]

Even if there are many glimmers of hope and signs of change, the uncomfortable truth remains that over 20 years on from the adoption of the Framework Convention on Climate Change at the Rio Earth Summit in 1992, a global turnaround is still a distant prospect — although our knowledge about climate change has grown and consolidated enormously in the meantime, resulting in a unique and historic agreement on the necessity to limit global warming to 2 °C above the preindustrial level and to "pursue efforts to limit temperature increase to 1.5 °C above pre-industrial levels" (Article 2, para. 1 [a] of the Paris Agreement). However, although the economic logic just as clearly supports the need for a rigorous climate policy, and massive efforts to expand renewable energies are being undertaken all over the world, our endeavours do not suffice.

2

The great loss
of biological diversity

"It is a document that should make the whole world sit up," UNEP Executive Director Achim Steiner said at the launch of the "Global Biodiversity Outlook" in October 2014. However, it seems to have missed its mark completely. The release of the report during the annual conference of the parties to the Convention on Biological Diversity was barely registered internationally, although the report makes clear that the condition of nature has deteriorated dramatically. The report underscores that climate change is not the only factor jeopardising the outlook for the global future. Apart from climate change, the loss of biodiversity has been identified as a further major and urgent global challenge. That is why the Convention on Biological Diversity (CBD) was adopted alongside the Framework Convention on Climate Change in Rio de Janeiro in 1992.

Since 1992 our knowledge about the loss of ecosystems and biodiversity has deepened. "Loss" appears euphemistic in the light of more recent research, in which the term "great extinction" has gained currency. The human-induced extinction of species is only comparable with the extinction that took place 250 million years ago (known as the "Permian-Triassic mass extinction") in which some 90 per cent of all animal and plant species disappeared. Indeed, the figures are alarming: new studies suggest that the current extinction rate is around 1000 times higher than in the pre-human era — and that the trend is rising.[25] According to the Living Planet Index the number of animals has diminished by around 52 per cent since 1970.[26]

The principal cause for the extinction of life forms is habitat loss due to the expansion of land take for human use — be it for agriculture, infrastructure and human settlements or large-scale projects such as dams or mining. Moreover, fish resources are overused globally, which also entails the destruction of coral reefs and mangroves and the discharge of toxic substances and excess nutrients into rivers and lakes.

The destruction of the extremely species-rich tropical rainforests is a particularly serious issue. Although only some seven per cent of ice-free land area is covered by rainforests, it is estimated that these are home to around 90 per cent of all animal and plant species, many of which are still unknown. The significance of species diversity for the sustainability of life on Earth cannot easily be verified — but we know that diversity is the foundation of evolution and biological development. Nevertheless, the destruction of rainforests accelerated between 2000 and 2010: an area the size of Germany was destroyed every five years.[27] In the Amazon region, the world's largest rainforest area, conversion into grazing lands and illegal logging are the main causes of deforestation; in Indonesia it is the establishment of palm oil plantations. The destruction of forests is not primarily the doing of poor small-scale farmers but of an export-oriented economy integrated into the global market.

The destruction of natural landscapes and the degradation of biodiversity is not just a problem in tropical climes but also in Germany. The report published by the German government in 2014 under the ambitious title "The State Of Nature" *(Zur Lage der Natur)* leaves no doubt about that. Habitat conservation is ranked as "inadequate" (39 per cent) or "poor" (31 per cent) in most regions of Germany. Likewise, only 25 per cent of regions achieve the rating "favourable" for species conservation. The reasons for this are diverse and in some cases are rooted specifically in current trends. For instance, the increased cultivation of maize for energy generation and rape for fuel production ("biodiesel") have contributed to the massive spread of monocultures.[28] Yet the subsidisation of biofuel is justified as a measure to combat climate change.

But it is not just the way in which land is used which threatens natural habitats: despite falling population figures, in Germany on average around 70 hectares of fertile soil per day is sealed over. In recent years, the land consumption figures have levelled out at this value following a slight drop (in 2000 it was still 129 hectares per day). Thus Germany is far from achieving its self-imposed target of reducing surface sealing to 30 hectares per day by 2020.[29] But instead of making soil-sealing more difficult, the German nature conservation authorities rely on what are known as land agencies ("Flächenagenturen"). The core of the impact mitigation regulation that has been in force since 1976 in German nature conservation is the compensation principle: where nature and landscape are impaired by new facilities, settlements or highways, the impact must be compensated. To this end, the land agencies "pool" suitable land parcels. These "land pools" (also known as "eco accounts") offer the opportunity to combine several individual measures onto comparatively large, contiguous land areas. Such an approach appears sensible at first glance. But the land pools are not a means of reducing land consumption; all they do is organise it. And by simplifying compensation, they may even become an instrument promoting land consumption.

As long ago as 2005, the UN published the Millennium Assessment with the objective of not only documenting the extent of natural destruction but also showing how important the conservation of biodiversity is for humans. It is not merely about the protection of appealing or rare animal species but the preservation of the very basis for the reproduction of life on our planet. The significance of biodiversity and the extent of destruction are well documented and hardly disputed; and if one considers colony collapse disorder in bees, for example, and the associated harvest losses due to lack of pollination, then the wider public, too, recognises how the loss of biodiversity and ecosystems can lead to fatal consequences. And yet, even in 2015, 23 years after the Rio Earth Summit, the state of endangered species has in no way improved.

3

Business as usual in agroindustry

The outlook on global agriculture has changed radically in the last decade. Into the 1990s, growth in production was outpacing demand. The prices of agricultural products were consistently low, leaving a correspondingly weak incentive for private investment in the sector. Despite huge subsidies in the industrialised countries, overall agricultural policy led a wallflower existence. The greatest problem at that time was how to deal with state-subsidised overproduction — the milk lakes and butter mountains in the USA and the EU. One way out was cheap exportation to developing countries. There, local prices and agricultural structures were (and continue to be) destroyed by the practice of cheap exports (such as exporting cheap poultry remnants).

Today, agriculture is at the centre of economic and political interests: land is more coveted and scarce and expensive than ever before. Prices of agricultural products have risen drastically since the turn of the millennium. The reason is that, today, demand is rising faster than production, compounded by the circumstance that oil prices rose sharply in the first half of the new millennium. By the year 2015, there will be nine to ten billion people needing to be nourished. The rising demand from the global middle classes for animal proteins from meat and milk clamours to be met before all else. Moreover, there is growing demand for biomass for energy generation and as an alternative industrial feedstock and substitute for petroleum, e.g. for chemical production. Yet it is not only the rise in prices which affects agriculture markets; currently it is also the great volatility of prices which negatively affects small and medium producers in particular. When oil prices fell sharply in 2015, prices for agricultural products followed. Even though growth in demand for agricultural products is still exploding, the prices for major oil-intensive agricultural inputs dropped steadily and the prices for agricultural products took the same trajectory. When oil prices are low the incentive to substitute fossil oil by agricultural products declines. This, in turn, decreases in the short term the demand pressure on markets and leads to decreasing prices. On the other hand, the discussions around the potential application of Bioenergy with Carbon Capture and Storage (BECCS) technologies to remove carbon from the atmosphere to create "negative emissions" to meet climate targets (see chapter 7) increases the pressure on land. Hence, there is no doubt about the drastically increasing demand for agricultural produce and land. The only open question is whether this will be at high or at low prices.

However, the expansion of agricultural production clashes with the limits of the available natural production factors: soil and land are very limited resources. The Earth has 13.4 billion hectares of land surface. Five billion hectares of this is agricultural land, which in turn breaks down into 1.45 billion hectares of arable land and 3.55 billion hectares of pasture land.[30] In newly industrialising and developing countries (hence mainly in tropical zones), arable land and pasture land have undergone massive expansion since the 1980s. The International Resource Panel of the UNEP estimates that under conditions of business as usual, between 320 and 849 million hectares of natural landscape must be converted into productive land by 2050.[31] According to a report from the United Nations Development Programme (UNDP) — assuming a continuing increase in land use — the limits to environmental carrying capacity will have been reached by 2020. If we carry on converting land into arable land as we have done — according to the UNEP Resource Panel — we will have exceeded "the safe operating space" by 2050 at the latest.

At the same time, despite massive inputs of fertilisers and pesticides, growth in production per hectare in many regions of the world has been in decline for years. In the 1980s, production growth per hectare was assumed to be three per cent on average. Today, the world-wide average is just a little over one per cent. On the one hand, the industrialised agricultural model is increasingly failing to deliver on its economic promises, while on the other, it is leaving behind a mire of environmental and social consequences. Natural ecosystems like primary forests, savannas and wetlands are disappearing; they are being converted into fields and plantations. In the process, the carbon stored in the soil over millennia is being released as CO_2 into the atmosphere. Added to this, the inappropriate use of nitrogen-based fertilisers is giving rise to nitrous oxide, a gas that is 365 times as harmful to the climate as CO_2; and both wet-rice agriculture and the intensive management of ruminants are giving rise to a growing source of greenhouse gases. Around 84 per cent of global N_2O (nitrous oxide) and 52 per cent of global CH_4 (methane) emissions originate from agriculture.[32]

However, biodiversity loss and the release of greenhouse gases are not all: intensified agriculture involving high inputs of fertilisers and pesticides pollutes waters and contaminates soils. Soil degradation and the loss of fertile soils through inappropriate soil cultivation are a serious problem today. Every year, 24 million tonnes of fertile soil are lost, which further exacerbates the prevailing scarcity of fertile land in many regions.[33] But instead of investing in soil fertility and choosing environmentally adapted cultivation methods, in many places the soil structure is being destroyed by massive inputs of nitrogen and laid wide open to wind and water erosion as a result of unsuitable production methods.

It takes several thousand years to accumulate a few centimetres of soil but just a few minutes of severe rainfall to wash it away again. Since fertile land is already scarce, it is all the more important to question why, for whom and how crops are produced: in order to provide healthy and balanced nutrition for all seven billion people, or principally for feedstuffs or biomass in order to obtain meat, energy and fuels to service the consumer requirements of the global middle classes and boost the profits and power of the agribusiness multinationals?

The expert panel appointed by UNEP calculated how much arable land we could use if it were shared fairly. The answer is 0.2 hectares per person per year — which is less than one-third of a football pitch and less than one-sixth of what every European currently consumes.

If the present trend in demand is maintained, today's meat consumption of 300 million tonnes will grow to 450 million tonnes by the year 2050. Today feedstuffs are produced on 33 per cent of the global arable land area, and if every person ate as much meat as an average European, then as much as 80 per cent of the world's available arable land would have to be used exclusively for meat production.

If the primary objective of agricultural production is food security and if we want to free millions of people from hunger, then we must halt and reverse this trend as the very top priority. Moreover, the use of arable products like maize or soya for industrial livestock production is highly inefficient: depending on the animal, the transformation ratio from plant into animal calories fluctuates between 2:1 for poultry, 3:1 for pigs and 7:1 for cows. Devoting fertile land to the production of feed crops on the current scale is sheer waste.

The production of feedstuffs for meat production and crops to produce agrofuels not only takes up huge areas of farmland domestically but also in other far-away countries. Europe is the continent that relies most heavily on land beyond its own borders. For instance, Europe imports around 35 million tonnes of soya per year for its intensive livestock production. This quantity, expressed in terms of land area, means that Europe is effectively "importing" between 15 and 17 million hectares, which roughly equates to Germany's entire agricultural land area. Overall, the European Union imports agricultural products grown on arable land outside the EU amounting to approximately 30 million hectares.

The result is that global competition for agricultural land is intensifying. One consequence is that small farmers are placed at a disadvantage, and the food sovereignty of the poorest of the poor is endangered.

Land – a contested resource

The competition for agricultural land is thus increasing the cost of land and leading to land grabbing, which leads in turn to the displacement of small farmers, nomads, etc. According to estimates, between the years 2000 and 2010 around 200 million hectares of land changed owners — five times more than the area of Germany.[34] Investors dispute over the land, which is actually being used by more than 500 million small-scale farmers, pastoralists and indigenous population groups. Expelled and cast out, they are forced to resort to less fertile land or move, completely impoverished, into the city without prospects or compensation. Conflicts over use also intensify local power disparities within social or ethnic groups; these are frequently resolved with violence. Because of a lack of land titles, as well as weak democratic structures, many of those affected barely have the resources or suitable avenues to defend their rights. In most countries they are only loosely politically organised, if at all. Neofeudal structures, dependency on loans, repression and intimidation amplify their powerlessness.

Who has access to land and who does not? The answer to this question is a reliable indicator of hunger. What most people do not know is that land is even more unequally distributed than income. Comparable data are available for 50 countries. Only in one of these countries, Côte d'Ivoire, is the distribution of land as unequal as the distribution of income. In all other countries the distribution of land is more unequal than that of income. In countries in which no more than two per cent of the population live from agriculture today, such as Germany for example, that is no problem because there are alternative sources of income. In many Asian and African countries, where it is common for more than 50 per cent of the population to live off the land and where there are barely social protection systems, lack of access to land is a certain predictor of hunger and poverty. Around 50 per cent of households affected by hunger are small farmers' families. Around 20 per cent of households where hunger is rife are landless.

The ever-intensifying competition between the production of food-stuffs, feedstuffs and energy crops is in full swing. The new growth promised by the Green Economy will further heighten this trend, as will the quest for negative emission technologies to compensate for the failure to quit our fossil fuel addiction. Fossil fuels like petroleum are expected to be replaced by renewable raw materials (biomass). The EU alone would need a further 70 million hectares of land if it is to fulfil the required shares of bioenergy pursuant to its adopted 2030 Climate and Energy Framework. This would amount to an area greater than the size of France. However, biofuels do not really relieve pressure on the climate: the energy "harvested" annually per square metre of bioenergy is, on average, just one-hundredth of the yield of wind or solar power plants.

The power of the agroindustrial lobby

The increasing demand for every form of biomass goes hand in hand with an enormous concentration of economic power, so that glob-ally just a few corporate groups dominate the agricultural sector and the food industry. In food production, in processing and most of all in global trade, corporations are continually expanding their market power. In particular, they are ruthlessly tightening control over central production factors — access to land, seed, pesticides, ferti-lisers and farm machinery (hardware and software) — which is con-centrated in the hands of just a few firms. On top of this comes legal control over land titles, water and intellectual property, such as seed rights, which is how it comes about that three corporations con-trol more than 50 per cent of the commercial seed market: Syngenta, Monsanto and DuPont Pioneer.[35] One single company, Monsanto, controls 41 per cent of the seed crop for commercial maize, one-quar-ter of the global seed crop for soya and supplies 90 per cent of all GM seed used in agriculture.[36] The Big Six (BASF, Bayer, Dow, DuPont, Monsanto, Syngenta), with collective revenues of more than $65 bil-lion in agrochemicals, seeds and biotech traits (2013 figures), control 75 per cent of the global agrochemical market, 63 per cent of the commercial seed market, and more than 75 per cent of all private sector research in seeds and pesticides.[37] Dow and DuPont teaming up and ChemChina purchasing Syngenta are only the beginning of a further concentration of market power. Safeguarding this market power in the long run is the goal of the powerful seed, fertiliser and pesticide lobby. Patenting and access to "intellectual property" are firm components of economic negotiations and countless bilateral trade agreements between industrialised, newly industrialising and developing countries. On top of that, the four companies that control 56 per cent of the $116 billion farm machinery industry, and who already have the robotics hardware, are acquiring the software (Big Data, satellite surveillance) technologies and are thinking about adding the bio-based software (seeds and pesticides) to their shopping cart.[38]

Corporate turnover and market power have also grown. For instance, the turnover of the American retail group Walmart in 2013, at 476 billion US dollars, is greater than the gross domestic product of the Philippines, a country with 100 million inhabitants (purchasing power parity adjusted).

With their oligopolies and monopolies — much the same as in the energy sector — the multinationals lobby successfully in the political arena, make themselves heard and see to it that their interests dominate national agricultural policies, EU agricultural policy and the policy of the relevant international organisations.

Departure from BAU in agriculture is possible

Politics must answer the question of how those who suffer from poverty and hunger can be strengthened so that they can produce sufficient food to escape the hunger and poverty trap. How can they manage to sustain this long term, taking account of the negative impacts of climate change? How can we limit the market power of the few agribusiness multinationals and seriously promote agroecological methods of production at long last? And how can consumption structures — especially meat production — be changed? Answers to these questions are not forthcoming, either from European governments or from those of many African, Asian and Latin American countries. A departure from "business as usual" in global agricultural policy is long overdue in view of the scarcity of land and the environmental and social consequences of industrial agriculture. Information and public awareness-raising about the global consequences of meat consumption are the prerequisite for a shift towards ethical and sustainable consumption patterns.

There are many approaches to a more equitable and sustainable agricultural sector, and good examples of how it might look. One example is agroecology, which is based on the wealth of experience and the traditional knowledge of small-scale farmers. This is not a "one size fits all" approach but one that accepts that agroecological systems are locally diverse and complex.

Diversity in the field, recycling and ground cover can stimulate a vital, fertile and active soil which is also capable of ensuring optimal water management. A study by Jules Pretty, dating from 2006, on agroecological production methods investigated 286 environmentally sustainable agriculture projects in 57 countries and found an average 79 per cent rise in harvest yields.[39]

Likewise the Global Agriculture Report (IAASTD) of 2009 emphasised the significance of agroecological farming. The report considers support for the world's more than 500 million small-scale farmers to be *the* central task of the future, if hunger and poverty are to be consigned to the past.[40]

One thing is certain: our manner of producing and consuming exceeds the ecological boundaries of our planet. We therefore need a fundamental policy shift — towards sustainable and equitable farming.

4

The world as we know it: inequality, poverty, hunger

The environmental crisis is inseparable from the social conditions of the present. It is playing out in a world of inequalities, in which extreme poverty defines millions of people's lives. There is not the slightest indication that the world is about to eradicate these inequalities: in the period from 1980 to 2002, during Capitalism's neoliberal expansion phase, inequality *between* countries reached a new zenith, as even the World Bank acknowledges.[41]

Looking at today's world, what can be observed is this: the roughly 20 per cent that make up the world's elites and middle classes are able to live well, consume and produce, because they do so at the expense of nature and of the poor and the poorest of the poor. It bears repeating: in recent times this wealthy class has also become established in the southern hemisphere, in countries deemed to be utterly poor just a few decades ago, like India and China, for example. But whether in the North or in the South — we collectively foist the consequences of this model of production and consumption onto the poorest of the poor, and onto future generations. This happens in Argentina and Brazil — just to cite another example at this point — when we appropriate land areas on a major scale to service growing global meat consumption or to produce feedstuffs, thereby displacing local farmers from their land and destroying the environment. Our way of life entails massive social and environmental consequences which others are left to bear, leading some researchers to designate it the "imperial mode of living".[42]

The structure of farming

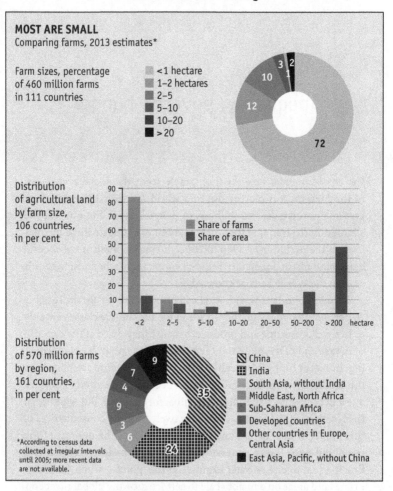

MOST ARE SMALL
Comparing farms, 2013 estimates*

Farm sizes, percentage
of 460 million farms
in 111 countries

- <1 hectare
- 1–2 hectares
- 2–5
- 5–10
- 10–20
- >20

3 2
10 1
12
72

Distribution
of agricultural land
by farm size,
106 countries,
in per cent

Share of farms
Share of area

<2   2–5   5–10   10–20   20–50   50–200   >200   hectare

Distribution
of 570 million farms
by region,
161 countries,
in per cent

9
7
4
9
3
6
35
24

- China
- India
- South Asia, without India
- Middle East, North Africa
- Sub-Saharan Africa
- Developed countries
- Other countries in Europe, Central Asia
- East Asia, Pacific, without China

*According to census data
collected at irregular intervals
until 2005; more recent data
are not available.

Most farms around the world are tiny—but governments seldom support
the needs of smallholders, even though they have the potential to make a
meaningful contribution to food security. Instead, ownership of fertile land
is increasingly being transferred—often through land grabbing—to agroindustrial trusts. Opposition to these acquisitions is growing, however.

Source: SOIL ATLAS – Facts and figures about earth, land and fields (www.boell.de)

Ecology is a top-ranking question of justice. Firstly, it concerns future generations being able to enjoy the same life chances; in other words, intergenerational justice. Secondly, inherent in the necessary reconfiguration of the industrial society, referred to by some as the Great Transformation, is an immense dimension of intra- and inter-societal justice.

How are energy prices formed or transport costs determined? Who is excluded by the various reconfiguration scenarios? Do they exacerbate inequality? Thirdly, it implies equitable compensation between the highly industrialised North, which has consumed the lion's share of natural resources hitherto and produced the lion's share of emissions, and the developing and newly industrialising countries, which are most severely affected by climate change and other environmental crises. Among other evidence, the multilateral climate negotiations testify to these lines of conflict.

All these are political questions that are tightly linked to power politics and special-interest lobbying within and between countries, and to democratic issues like participation, transparency and gender equity. To whom do resources belong? Who determines who has access to them? Who profits from sustainable development and whose interests does it serve? These are crucial questions for the present day and the future.

In the meantime, the greatest problem — which has likewise worsened in the last three decades — is the inequality within societies. "Seven out of ten people live in countries where the gap between rich and poor is greater than it was 30 years ago", wrote Oxfam in an extensive report on global inequality. Thomas Piketty and Lucas Chancel show that one tenth of people are responsible for 45 per cent of global emissions. These are luxury emissions and should be cut first. These top ten per cent live across the globe — one third of them in developing countries.[43]

Back in 2010, the wealth amassed by the world's 388 richest people equalled the wealth of the poorest 50 per cent of the world population (3.5 billion people); in 2014, the same share was in the hands of just 80 people. And in 2015 62 people owned just as much as half of the world's population! Just nine of the 62 are women. Oxfam's pre-diction—made ahead of the 2015 Davos gathering—that one per cent would soon own more than the rest of us by 2016, actually came true in 2015, a year early.[44]

It is the newly industrialising countries in which the income and asset disparities are especially high: Brazil, India, Indonesia, South Africa, Russia and Turkey.[45]

Inequality has many dimensions, and is not confined merely to income and property relations. Access to resources is also unequal in the extreme. To illustrate this once again in the context of access to land: the bulk of all agricultural enterprises worldwide, namely 72 per cent, farm on less than one hectare of land, while only two per cent of holdings manage more than 20 hectares.[46] Nevertheless, these two per cent manage more than 60 per cent of all the agricultural land world-wide. To produce the products consumed by an average European, it takes around 1.3 hectares of land per year. That is around six times more than someone in Bangladesh has at their disposal. Moreover, almost 60 per cent of the land in use to satisfy European consumption is located outside the EU.

Land grabbing is only the most visible form of this appropriation. The extreme inequality affecting access to land and resources is a fun-damental dimension for all debates on growth: while for some ad-equate access has yet to be secured, the critical question for others is how a good life is possible with any less access to resources.

Yet our world is not just afflicted by inequalities but also by bitter poverty and hunger. Worldwide, almost one person in every seven is affected by hunger. That is almost one billion people, and a fur-ther billion are malnourished and undernourished. Three-quarters of the hungry live in rural regions, and women make up the bulk of this population, accounting for 60 per cent. As a proportion of its popula-tion, the African continent has the highest rates of hunger.

In countries like India and China, too, a notable share of the popu-lation still lives with hunger. According to data from the Global Hun-ger Index, in China 22.9 per cent of the population are undernour-ished, and as many as 25.5 per cent in India.[47] At the same time, one fact applies worldwide: people who are hungry are socially and polit- ically marginalised in their societies.

It is a truism that economic growth per se is no guarantee that hunger, poverty and inequality will be wiped out. For that to happen, power structures must be changed and redistribution organised so that it becomes possible for the population to participate in economic growth. Productivity gains alone, and especially the steps taken to achieve them, such as agricultural high-tech, commercial seed and still more chemical fertilisers etc., have not succeeded in eradicating world hunger.

The reason why so many poor people in rural areas are affected, women most of all, is the lack of access to adequate resources like land, water and fertilisers to produce sufficient food for themselves, but also a lack of money to buy themselves adequate food. The absence of land titles, and hence the lack of secure rights of ownership, use and disposal over property, presents a major problem in most develop- ing countries. Differentials in power and rights of ownership between the genders are a key factor explaining why women make up the bulk of the hungry. They are also frequently excluded by inheritance law.

Often the inequality is ignored and attention steered towards a dif- ferent dynamic: global population growth. The very word "popula- tion explosion" and the figure of nine billion — the estimated pop- ulation in the year 2050 — can immediately conjure up a terrifying scenario. Yet the problem is not the stated number of people, but rather the per-capita consumption of resources by the wealthy and the middle classes worldwide. Incidentally, the majority of forecasts indicate that, from 2050, the number of people in the world will stabi- lise or even decline. In many regions of the world, even today, shrink- age of the population figure is far more of a problem than any in- crease.[48] According to one of the possible scenarios elaborated by the population section of the UN Department of Economic and Social Affairs (UNDESA), the world population might reach its peak by around 2050 and begin to fall from that time onwards, first slowly and then ever faster.[49] So it is misleading to talk about ecological boundaries without including the social dimension.

The doughnut of social and planetary boundaries

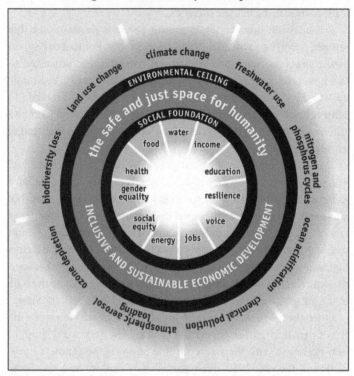

GDP growth, as an economic indicator of wealth, is not up to the task of capturing the complex social and environmental challenges facing the world in the 21st century. Economist Kate Raworth from Oxford University has developed a visual framework—shaped like a doughnut—which combines the concept of planetary boundaries with the complementary concept of human rights. The planetary boundaries form the outer ring of the doughnut, while the inner ring consists of standards of social justice which must be adhered to. The success of an economic system should be measured not only in financial and material terms but also by the extent to which it respects these boundaries and takes the environment, unpaid care and social inequalities fully into account.

Source: Kate Raworth, A safe and just space for humanity: Can we live within the doughnut?, *Oxfam Discussion Paper, Oxford, inspired by Röckstrom et al. (2009),* A safe operating space for humanity, Nature *461, 472–475; http://www.kateraworth. com/doughnut/*

The economist Kate Raworth from Oxford University therefore enlarged upon the "planetary boundaries" approach with an important added dimension: that of social justice. Here, the safe space in which humankind can survive in peace and justice while respecting natural boundaries is shown in the form of a doughnut.[50] Raworth explains that policies should be framed so as to release those from the poverty trap who fall into the hole in the doughnut by giving them more access to and control over natural resources and by safeguarding their human rights. At the same time, however, those whose colossal ecological footprints (and immense resource consumption due to the imperial mode of living) catapult us beyond the rim of the doughnut should be brought back into the middle by means of redistribution. It is self-evident to Raworth that this is only conceivable if the mania for growth is rejected altogether. We will come back to this later.

5

The Green Economy as
a way out of the global crisis?

"Business as usual" is not a realistic option, as even the international mainstream of the World Bank, UNEP and OECD acknowledge, an admission which has in turn boosted the Green Economy's career prospects. Breaking away from "more of the same" is the prerequisite for all conceptual and practical Green Economy approaches.

What form a departure from business as usual should take is a contentious matter. For nobody has defined what is meant by Green Economy—and certainly not in international law—thus leaving it open to divergent or even contradictory interpretations. The original "Green Economy" idea is somewhat vague. Nevertheless, a discourse has grown up and become established around the concept and is making an impact.

Up to the year 2008, the concept was used very little, and if it was, then mainly in the context of Green movements and political parties. As early as 1999, for instance, the economics professor and current British Green Party member of the European Parliament, Molly Scott Cato, published a book entitled *Green Economics*. For Cato, green economics is "inherently concerned with social justice. [...] Green economics has emerged from environmental campaigners and Green politicians because of their need for it. It has grown from the bottom up and from those who are building a sustainable economy in practice rather than from abstract theories."[51]

Soon, however, the conception drifted away from its grassroots origins. Initially, the concept that rose to popularity in the context of the financial and economic crisis from 2008 onward, was the "Green New Deal". Green growth was expected to provide an answer both to the economic crisis and to global environmental challenges. In 2009, the United Nations Environment Programme, UNEP, launched the initiative for a "Global Green New Deal". Achim Steiner, the Executive Director of UNEP, has become an eloquent and committed advocate of that conception. In the same year, the US President Barack Obama pledged to support a "Green New Deal", while in Germany this concept found its way into the election manifesto of the German Green Party (Bündnis 90/Die Grünen). The idea of the "Green New Deal" harks back to historical experiences in the USA in the 1930s and 1940s, and hence to a neo-Keynesian tradition, whereby increasing government expenditure — financed by borrowing if need be — is seen as an appropriate response to economic crises. At this juncture, proposals for "greening" the economy and adherence to the pivotal significance of economic growth entered into a marriage that would prove to be enduring.

Prior to and during the Rio+20 Conference in 2012, "Green Economy" conceptions were then developed by three key actors: UNEP, the World Bank and OECD. The Green Economy was developed not so much as a new approach in economic theory, but rather as an attempt to lay new foundations for global environmental policy twenty years after the 1992 Rio Conference.

The search for a new paradigm had surely been encouraged by the general perception that "sustainable development" felt timeworn and largely devoid of content. Furthermore, the term "development" steered attention heavily towards the so-called "developing countries". The new concept of Green Economy would finally address all countries, calling attention to their responsibility. Another thing that had changed was the role of economics, in the perception of many actors. The Stern Review was and is adjudged by many to have been a near-Copernican revolution in the climate debate. The former World Bank Chief Economist, Sir Nicolas Stern, had published a study in 2006 commissioned by the British government, which was intended to show that a resolute and rapid climate policy actually made economic sense, because inaction itself would turn out to be even more expensive. This economic study of climate change was to contribute immensely to the mainstreaming of climate policy. And indeed, climate policy made the leap out of its environmental niche into the heart of the economy. At the same time, Stern's analysis made it possible to consider environmental policy as an opportunity for new investments — investments that would result in more cost savings than they would actually cost.

This is essentially the decisive conceptual innovation which was and continues to be expanded into a more encompassing Green Economy approach. Economic rationality no longer contradicts environmental and climate policy; on the contrary, it fosters it. This is no trivial promise.

The approach of incorporating nature into economic thinking highlights a further precursor of Green Economy in the history of economic theory. The criticism that economics disregarded nature was practically a leitmotiv of "Ecological Economics", the critique of classical economics by a generation of environmentally-oriented economists whose best known representatives are surely Herman Daly and Robert Costanza. The ecological critique accused classical economics of perceiving the environment and nature primarily as external factors, and hence consigning them to systematic neglect. The insistence on the internalisation of external factors — by means of an "eco-tax", for instance — became one of the key reference points in the relationship between environmental policy and economics.

Various international initiatives, particularly the World Bank, took up some of the fundamental ideas of this Ecological Economics, systematised them and brought them up to date. The inclusion of nature in economics becomes a key question in this context. For nature and economics to be able to communicate with each other, however, data about nature needs to be captured in a way that is comprehensible to economics. That means nature must be quantified and, if possible, framed in monetary values. Hence the question of quantifying and measuring "natural capital" is a crucial unresolved issue of Green Economy which we will go on to explore thoroughly.

For an understanding of the Green Economy, however, one other development of recent decades is important. The tough negotiation process in relation to the Framework Convention on Climate Change, in particular, has done much to diminish hopes of an international climate regime that sets globally accepted and ambitious threshold values for greenhouse gases. The Paris Agreement buried that hope — if not forever at least for the foreseeable future. Another disappointment is the second convention that was adopted at the 1992 Earth Summit, the Convention on Biological Diversity. It did not succeed in halting the megatrend of biodiversity destruction; many of its resolutions were not implemented. This policy failure reinforces ideas that place more emphasis on a change of course through economic incentives than on regulations. Within the UN system, efforts to involve the business sector have been intensifying for some time. The most prominent example is the Global Compact, i.e. the initiative that attempts to recruit corporations to adhere, on a voluntary basis, to such standards as human rights principles and labour norms. The Secretary General of the United Nations, Ban Ki-moon, summarises this as follows: "To a growing extent we do not consider business as a problem but as the place we must go to when we want to find solutions."[52]

All these developments are the backdrop against which the systematisation into a Green Economy approach is taking place. Or as Pavan Sukhdev puts it: "Economics has become the currency of politics."[53] The world of global environmental policy does indeed look different in 2012 than in 1992.

Against this backdrop, the UNEP, World Bank and OECD launched their Green Economy conceptions. UNEP in particular strongly advocated using the Rio+20 Conference to establish Green Economy as a new global paradigm in order to replace or at least augment the "sustainable development" paradigm, which had come to look very threadbare. This was not a complete success. Green Economy did not spark a global love affair at the 2012 conference in Brazil; instead, reactions to Green Economy from actors from the global South, representing both governmental and non-governmental interests, ranged from sceptical to hostile.

That is another point which should not be overlooked: Green Economy has become a negatively charged concept for many critical actors. Thus, the closing declaration of the People's Summit convened by civil society groups as an alternative to the Rio +20 conference contains an explicit rejection of this conception. As annoying or baffling as this may be for all those who want to uphold an emphatic concept of Green Economy, it must nevertheless be borne in mind. In particular, the Green Economy approach of including nature as "natural capital" in economic calculations prompted the objection that it was "mercantilising nature". Actors from the South contributed quite different conceptions to the debate, such as the "right to good living" (buen vivir) anchored in the constitutions of Bolivia and Ecuador, or the appeal to grant rights to nature (Mother Earth) itself. Ever since Rio, if not before, Green Economy has turned into a bone of contention, a disputed concept.

The versions presented by UNEP, OECD and the World Bank are complex, and diverge on certain points. For instance, UNEP places especially strong emphasis on the dimension of social justice. Nevertheless, a few fundamental trends are common to all the approaches. The message is, Green Economy and growth belong together; this is etched into the heart and the DNA of Green Economy. Likewise, the UNEP, which has developed perhaps the most differentiated Green Economy approach, promises that this will not only generate growth but actually stronger GDP growth. Green Economy, it is claimed, could become a "new engine of growth".[54] Rachel Kyte, Vice President of the World Bank, is categorical: "To talk about anything other than how to grow is a non-starter."[55]

Such choices of phrasing also make it clear that Green Economy is to be discussed less as a theoretical conception and more as a pragmatically conceived policy approach. The pivotal role of the growth promise is what differentiates the Green Economy conception from other approaches, distinguishing it particularly from all those approaches which see growth as problematic. The most important global actors in the debate have meanwhile joined forces to form a "Green Growth Knowledge" platform: this unites the OECD, UNEP, World

Green economy – defining terms
*(The following definition is taken from a
Green Growth Knowledge Platform Scoping Paper)*

"Green growth and green economy have been subject to various definitions but those currently being used by international organisations have a lot in common. Green growth seeks to fuse sustainable development's economic and environmental pillars into a single intellectual and policy planning process, thereby recasting the very essence of the development model so that it is capable of producing strong and sustainable growth simultaneously [...]. It aims to foster economic growth and development, while ensuring that natural assets are used sustainably, and continue to provide the resources and environmental services on which the growth and well-being rely [...]. It is growth that is efficient in its use of natural resources, clean in that it minimises pollution and environmental impacts and resilient in that it accounts for natural hazards [...]. Green economy aims for improved human well-being and social equity, while significantly reducing environmental risks and ecological scarcities [...]. The concept of green economy rests on the economy, the environment and the social pillars of sustainable development. A broader concept of 'inclusive' green growth or sustainable development incorporates fully the social sustainability aspects, in particular enhancing human development and the conditions for the poor and vulnerable."[56]

Bank and the Global Green Growth Institute (headquartered in South Korea). It is striking that the concept of Green Growth is now gaining the upper hand. Indeed, from the very start, all Green Economy conceptions have been intimately linked with adherence to the special significance of growth.[57] Green Economy and Green Growth have melded into a pair of concepts which have become almost interchangeable.

The second constitutive element for the Green Economy conception is the proposition, already implicit in the coining of the term, that the decisive challenge is not political but economic. "Economics first" is the message; the main thing is to get the economics right. The notion, which gained huge popularity thanks to the Stern Report, that climate change is the greatest market failure in history, culminates in the following point: if that be the case, then the critical challenge is to correct this market failure, and to do so with more market. This extends the horizon far beyond a more efficient, resource-saving economy.

The challenge of reconciling economics and ecology with growth calls for a wide-ranging systemic transformation. "To get the economies right" is not a banal task. A fundamental priority in this process is to capture the economic value of nature as natural capital. But this, in itself, is the point of principle that underlies the sometimes very vehement criticism of the Green Economy conception.

A further pillar of Green Economy is the development of strategies and technologies for the better use of natural resources. Innovation thus represents a central hope and closely connects the Green Economy conception with bioeconomy approaches. The German government's Green Economy research agenda emphasises this connection explicitly: "Whilst the bioeconomy uses and further develops biological processes and resources and in doing so makes them more efficient, technology, economy and ecology are systemically and sustainably linked — in line with the aims and guidelines of a Green Economy."[58]

The switch from fossil fuels to biomass, the use of new biotechnologies and the integration of "ecosystem services" in the economy are central concerns of the bioeconomy. The pivotal element of the bioeconomy is its faith in technological solutions (the "techno fix").

Likewise, the Green Economy transformation agenda is founded, firstly, on a re-orientation of the economy entailing the integration of nature, and, secondly, on faith in technological solutions. Without the miraculous power of innovation, the promises of green growth are unfulfillable.

The aspects cited here are the critical leverage points of the various Green Economy approaches. Green Economy does contain a range of positive elements and does state a few key challenges accurately, for example, how to supersede the fossil age and move urgently towards a low-emission and resource-efficient future. But the decisive question is whether Green Economy is developing the right strategies. Only after realising that "business as usual" is not an option does the debate begin about *how* to effectuate the necessary social and environmental transformation — and the question of *whose* need of it is especially pressing.

On occasion, further confusion is added to the debate when Green Economy is criticised on the basis of mistaken arguments. By no means all protagonists of the old ("brown") economy have now become fervent or dubious Green Economy disciples. Specifically because it involves getting to grips with concrete strategies, climate policy will occupy a special position in our critical study, for that is the setting in which global approaches towards a new economy of nature are being developed and implemented most promisingly. In this connection we view the *New Climate Economy Report*,[59] published in 2014 by the Global Commission on the Economy and Climate, as an important example of the new economic approaches for global climate and environmental policy.

PART TWO

Rampant risk: questionable instruments and innovations

6

Nature or natural capital?

Green Economy sets out to rectify the failure of classical economics witnessed with regard to climate change and biodiversity loss by assigning a monetary value to nature and by integrating ecosystem services into the market system. Quantifying (accounting), appropriating and offsetting are the key methods of this route out of the climate and biodiversity crisis.

Quantification: accounting natural assets

Perhaps the most succinct expression of economic failure with regard to nature comes from Pavan Sukhdev: "We use nature because it's valuable, but we lose it because it is free."[60] With this remark, Sukhdev places the question of the "value of nature" at the heart of the debate about a Green Economy. The "value" concept is ambiguous and does not necessarily denote a monetary value. But for an economic valuation, the question of price is central. And there is no price on natural assets such as clean air; this is inferred to be the reason for their over-exploitation or the root cause of their degradation. The World Bank expresses it as follows: "For economists, greener growth is fundamentally about changing the incentives that have led to environmental degradation and depletion — that is, 'getting the prices right.'"[61] For that to happen, prices must exist. Consequently, it argues: "Putting a monetary value on natural ecosystems is a key step on the road to 'green' economic growth."[62]

The fact that natural assets are not priced leads to a "misallocation of capital", according to UNEP. The great challenge of Green Economy is therefore to integrate into economic calculations and price systems the natural assets that economics has not previously taken into account.

The conceptual basis for this is a reframing of the concept of nature — as opposed to any transformation of our mode of production and consumption. The main implication associated with "rethinking economics" is "redefining nature". The task that immediately arises is that of developing methods, techniques and measurement procedures with which nature can now be valued and accounted for in economic terms. And, if the non-valuation of nature in economic terms has been the cause of its degradation up to now, then, within this logic, the solutions and intervention approaches concentrate specifically on the economisation of ecosystem services and nature's resources. As a result, many structural causes of the crisis of nature and climate change become invisible, and are no longer given extensive consideration in the search for solutions and ways out. An extremely complex constellation of problems is reduced to bare essentials. This is always accompanied by a "rendering invisible" of complex realities.

Fundamentals for the redefinition of nature, then, are its measurability and the (monetary) valorisation of its "services" (on this, see the following chapters). This process gives rise to new forms of appropriation of nature, practised mainly by those intent upon offsetting the destruction of one ecosystem against another, or numerous others, in order to justify "business as usual" despite planetary boundaries. Here, the social bonds, the existing relationships between humans and nature (and humans as part of nature) are mainly disregarded, although they are massively affected by the new forms of appropriation.

In economic analyses and political statements on Green Economy, the concept of *natural capital* is increasingly becoming established. As a conception it is extremely broadly framed, and perhaps this is also a source of difficulties and misunderstandings in the course of the somewhat heated debate about the financialisation of nature.

What is natural capital?

"Natural capital is the extension of the economic notion of capital […] to environmental goods and services. A functional definition of capital in general is: 'a stock that yields a flow of valuable goods or services into the future'. Natural capital is thus the stock of natural ecosystems that yields a flow of valuable ecosystem goods or services into the future. For example, a stock of trees or fish provides a flow of new trees or fish, a flow which can be sustainable indefinitely. Natural capital may also provide services like recycling wastes or water catchment and erosion control. Since the flow of services from ecosystems requires that they function as whole systems, the structure and diversity of the system are important components of natural capital."[63] The World Bank's definition is more concise: "But what exactly is natural capital? The term refers to the stock of natural resources that provides flows of valuable goods and services."[64]

Natural capital encompasses, first and foremost, "the stock" of natural assets, which includes things like mineral resources. The crucial point, however, is that this stock provides services such as air and water filtration. For this reason, "natural capital accounting" (NCA) normally aims both to record the stock and value the "flow", i.e. the services rendered by natural capital. In this way, for instance, not only a country's forested area (is it expanding, is it contracting?) but also service provided by this forest in storing CO_2 can be included in NCA.[65]

Natural capital erodes or is continuously destroyed by human influence. In the language of the new economics of nature, this environmental crisis is viewed as follows: "The startling erosion of our natural capital base will become the defining 21st century challenge facing every business. Natural capital is the foundation that supports human society, all economic activity and every business. The decline in this capital base, if left unchecked, will wreak havoc on business and society as we know it" — reads the emphatic warning of Ernst & Young LLP, one of the world's largest accountancy corporations.[66]

This purely economic view of nature entices and recruits — so it seems — new members into the alliance for the protection of "natural capital". The Natural Capital Coalition is a global multi-stakeholder platform whose participants include the World Bank, UNEP, the World Business Council for Sustainable Development and universities as well as numerous corporations and environmental organisations. This is how it views natural capital: "There are no extra planets. And as such we are using up the capital provided by nature rapidly and borrowing the remainder from the future. That is unsustainable. It is time that Natural Capital is taken on board in business and that its value is accounted for. This holds as much true for governments as for business. To bring Natural Capital into the systems that govern our businesses and companies, we will need the tools to calculate their worth, both in monetary and non-monetary terms."[67]

The title of a 2006 essay by Morgan Robertson, an American ecologist, who worked for the American Wetland Banking Scheme on the monetary valuation of wetlands, neatly encapsulates what is at stake: "The nature that capital can see."[68] For only what is visible to the economic eye counts as "nature". This calls for clearly quantifiable natural capital metrics. In the meantime, a significant constellation of actors has formed worldwide and is tackling this complex task. A Natural Capital Declaration drafted at the Rio+20 Conference in 2012 was signed by governments, financial sector institutions, corporations and NGOs. Among the objectives of the above-mentioned Natural Capital Coalition is the drafting of a Natural Capital Protocol that will be launched in 2016. The World Bank also brought the Waves Initiative into being ("Waves" stands for Wealth Accounting and Valuation of Ecosystem Services). Whereas the objective of Waves is to support countries in new approaches to accounting for natural capital, the Natural Capital Coalition is aimed more at an international standardisation of methods.

An important milestone on the path to a "natural capital account-ing" mechanism is the UN System of Environmental Economic Ac-counting (SEEA), which has developed an internationally agreed standard for biophysical *quantification* of natural resources. "SEEA Experimental Ecosystem Accounting has been developed within the broader process of revising the SEEA-2003 — a process initiated by the United Nations Statistical Commission (UNSC) in 2007. The pri-mary objective of the SEEA revision process was the establishment of a statistical standard for environmental-economic accounting. At its 43rd meeting in February 2012, the UNSC adopted the SEEA Central Framework as an initial international statistical standard for envi-ronmental-economic accounting."[69] The UN SEEA system therefore lays the foundation stone for a "statistical framework to measure en-vironment and its interaction with economy".[70] The SEEA's biophys-ical quantification is not synonymous with monetisation but stands as a comprehensive, global approach to making nature quantifiable and comparable.

The insistence that natural capital — to maintain this linguistic convention — is being disregarded is an old and plausible critique of traditional economic metrics, particularly gross domestic product (GDP). The GDP indicator does not take account of the degradation of nature or of natural capital, for example. Hence, it would certainly make sense not only to take into account fish consumption but also the development of fish stocks. Because gross domestic product fails to consider damage to the environment or even to value it positively, the natural capital accounting approach is highly plausible — at least at first glance.

Natural capital can be entered in the books in different ways, for example, by accounting for instances of damage to natural capital. In environmental economics, this is known as the valuation of externali-ties and has filtered through to mainstream economists. A good exam-ple of an external effect is air pollution. It can be regulated by means of statutory measures like banning lead in petrol, or else through pricing, perhaps in the form of a tax. In the debate about environmental harms and the use of economic mechanisms to combat these, this idea has been summed up in the catchy slogan: "The prices must tell the eco-logical truth." While this seems plausible or even persuasive at first, it still throws up a series of questions: For instance, does 20 cents more on the price of a litre of petrol tell the whole "truth" about petroleum and transport? (We will go into ambiguities regarding the "internalisation of external effects" more extensively later.)

However, the "natural capital" conception opens up yet another perspective for redefining the relationship of economics and nature and the valorisation of its resources. In recent years, functions of nature such as CO_2 storage in forests or soils have increasingly been described and conceptually framed as services provided by ecosystems. Now these "ecosystem services" are similarly being eyed up for economic valuation.

The conception of "natural capital" and "natural capital accounting" unifies these two strands of economic valuation of nature—the pricing of negative externalities and the valuation of ecosystem services. The debate surrounding the assessment of economic mechanisms in the context of Green Economy is often muddled because the various forms of valorisation and pricing are not distinguished clearly enough.[71]

The "natural capital" concept enters nature, as we have said, into the dimensions of the economy: nature can and will be described and accounted for in economic terms. The great failure of traditional economics indeed was and is that it never came close to accomplishing this. Now Green Economy hopes to assist by making it easier to account for nature; which means that nature must become easier to measure. The old, familiar maxim that "we can only manage what we measure", modulated into variants like "we can only treasure what we measure", has become a paradigmatic theme (almost a mantra) of Green Economy. In today's world, data that can be expressed in euros and dollars are becoming more and more important. This leads us to the other important mechanism in the economisation of nature: to *monetisation*, i.e. determining monetary values.

Monetisation – a contentious issue

Capturing the economic value of nature by means of *quantification* and *monetisation* has turned into a contentious issue politically. The fronts have become relatively entrenched. While one side sees great danger in both procedures, the other declares the economic valuation of nature to be the key to an about-turn in the direction of a rational Green Economy. The British journalist George Monbiot brought the debate and the critique of monetisation into focus in a brilliant article: failure of the markets is set to be remedied by more market mechanisms and monetisation. Monbiot dismisses this as the "neoliberal road to ruin".[72] There are some interesting responses to Monbiot, including those from two important protagonists of eco-economics, Robert Costanza and Herman Daly.[73] Their critique helps to elucidate important elements of this debate. For Costanza it is clear: "The valuation of ecosystems is not something we can choose to do or not do. Far from being impossible, it is happening every day, all the time, every time we make a decision that involves trade-offs that affect ecosystems. The problem is that this valuation is implicit in the decision, not explicit and transparent, and generally ignores the benefits from ecosystems. We are better off trying to pull back the curtain, messy and imperfect as that process might be."[74]

Here, Costanza articulates probably the most widespread objection to critiques of the natural capital approach, and quite rightly points out that valorisation is not synonymous with monetisation. "Valuation is about communicating trade-offs and the units chosen to express these trade-offs are arbitrary and depend on how well they communicate. We could use money, energy, time, land area or oranges as the common denominator. Money communicates trade-offs well because most people use money for this purpose (and they don't use energy, land or oranges)."

That is an important point: under present-day conditions — some would say: under capitalism — money is the central means of communication — and more. To be able to account for nature effectively in economic terms, monetisation is not just one random option among many, but an essential one. For that very reason, economic valorisation is a potential pitfall.[75]

Herman Daly's reply takes quite a different line. He argues that natural capital is not originally aimed at capturing nature in monetary terms: "The word 'capital' derives from 'capita' meaning 'heads', referring to heads of cattle in a herd. The herd is the capital stock; the sustainable annual increase in the herd is the flow of useful goods or 'income' yielded by the capital stock — all in physical, not monetary, terms. The same physical definition of natural capital applies to a forest that gives a sustainable yield of cut timber, or a fish population that yields a sustainable catch. This use of the term 'natural capital' is based on the relations of physical stocks and flows, and is independent of prices and monetary valuation."[76] Nevertheless, the majority of people who hear the term "natural capital" are unlikely to think of a herd of cattle.

For Daly and others, the term "natural capital" is important because it makes clear how fundamental it is to preserve the stock, i.e. the natural base of life and the economy — in line with the old saying that if you kill the milk cow for meat, there will be no more milk. But Daly is highly aware of the danger that the concept is increasingly passing into monetary-economic use, and spells out the fundamental distinction: "Money is fungible, natural stocks are not". Exactly. However, this fundamental distinction is glossed over in the economising language of natural capital. Nature is described in terms of economic categories; this is the point — and the problem.

"The environment is part of the economy and needs to be properly integrated into it so that growth opportunities will not be missed". This statement was originally made by Dieter Helm, Chairman of the British Natural Capital Committee. Monbiot (see above) quotes him in order to demonstrate the dangerous implications of the natural capital approach. In that approach, nature must be appropriately integrated into the economy, not the other way around. In this case, Daly refuses to follow — and this is where opinions diverge. The economy is turned into the whole and ecology into a subsystem. The integration of nature into the economy, however, calls for a particular version of nature that can communicate with the economy. Quantification need not be carried out solely in monetary values, but within the economic system monetary quantification is obviously the method that is most readily communicable. Hence, monetisation is not one kind of communication among many, but the quintessential mechanism.

This debate may appear unduly theoretical and perhaps even pointless to some. Yet these essential mechanisms of the economisation of nature are being applied and are having an influence in two of the most important intervention areas of the global environmental crisis, namely climate change and biodiversity loss. The debate is relevant to practice and has direct implications for humans and the rest of nature.

Climate change –
accounting, appropriating, offsetting

One of the oldest and most successful initiatives in the quantification of "natural capital" is the Carbon Disclosure Project (CDP). "Worldwide 722 institutional investors, holding a total of 87 trillion US dollars in assets (Dec. 2013)" have signed up with the CDP.[77] However, the CDP also attracts support from NGOs like the World Wide Fund for Nature (WWF). One of the CDP's key aims is to establish common standards for the measurement of CO_2, co-operating with other organisations like the World Resources Institute and the World Business Council for Sustainable Development.

Such a standardisation of methods and measuring techniques is urgently necessary because, in spite of a variety of difficulties and a collapse in prices, the international trade in CO_2 reduction certificates has now reached a substantial volume. According to World Bank data, in 2013 global CO_2 markets reached a volume of 30 billion US dollars.[78]

With regard to measurability and quantification, CO_2 has become something of a pioneer, not least because CO_2 is easier to measure than, for instance, ecosystem services. Today, CO_2 is largely commensurable, and thus complex processes connected with CO_2 emissions can now be reduced to a few statistics.

This is by no means addressed merely to CO_2; the global warming potential of other gases is similarly expressed in terms of CO_2, as a metric of the relative effect of the contribution to climate change. Global warming potential is thus a statement of how much a defined quantity of a greenhouse gas contributes to global warming. Carbon dioxide serves merely as a comparison value; the abbreviation is CO_{2e} (for "equivalent"). The value describes the average warming effect over a certain period of time, often referenced to 100 years. An example: Methane has a CO_2 equivalent of 25, meaning that in the first 100 years after its release into the atmosphere, a kilogram of methane contributes 25 times as much to climate change as a kilogram of CO_2. This makes it possible to compare the impacts of different greenhouse gases—although this impact comparison relates solely to the global warming effect and not to other consequences associated with the emission of the gas in question such as land-use changes, political power shifts, economic path dependencies, social conflicts, etc.

The surest course – a price for CO_2

In the efforts to value natural capital in terms of money, the price of CO_2 is a pivotal factor. CO_2 is not a commodity just like any other. Nobody can simply sell the CO_2 emissions from their private car, for instance—not even eBay can help with that. CO_2 is a greenhouse gas, i.e. a pollutant, or in economic terms: a negative externality. The establishment of CO_2 markets has created a new global paradigm: a "negative externality" has a price and can be traded—far beyond limited regional contexts. CO_2 pricing and emissions trading systems have become by far the most important beacons of hope for a general decarbonisation of the economy. CO_2 has decisive advantages for this role: it can be measured relatively well, a market already exists, and climate policy has already made the reduction of CO_2 its central reference point. But CO_2 has a further characteristic, which is often overlooked or neglected by many who pragmatically advocate CO_2 markets as an efficient environmental policy instrument. CO_2 is created both by the burning of fossil fuels (oil, coal and gas) and by the destruction of forests. In particular, forests, other biomass and soils can also function as CO_2 sinks. Thus, the measurement and pricing of CO_2 is virtually the ideal-typical realisation of the idea of natural capital. It combines the greenhouse gas emissions released by industry and by functions of nature (storage of CO_2) in a standard metric (emitted or avoided CO_2) — a step whose paradigmatic significance can not be overstated. In this way, the efforts of an indigenous community in the Amazon to reduce deforestation become commensurable (fungible) with the emissions of a cement factory in northern Europe — and potentially tradable.

Wolfgang Sachs says that "a history of environmental policy as the history of forgotten alternatives has not yet been written".[79] What he means is this: At the Earth Summit in Rio de Janeiro in 1992, a "silver bullet" was found to tackle climate change: reducing CO_2 emissions. This deflected political attention away from the causes of climate change and allowed policy makers to deal only with the symptoms in the form of emissions. Secondly, a decision was made to express climate change in units of calculation known as "CO_2 equivalents". CO_2, methane and other greenhouse gases such as nitrous oxide have very different qualities when it comes to their warming potential or the number of years they remain in the atmosphere. They also appear in specific natural surroundings and interact with local ecosystems and economies in different ways. Expressing all of these different qualities and potential impacts in one standard number reduces a very complex problem to something that policy makers feel they can deal with through a single solution, policy, instrument and target. A third wrong turn was to offset emissions from the burning of fossil fuels against those from biological processes involving land, plants and animals.

Against this backdrop it can come as no surprise that "putting a price on carbon" has become a key question in global climate policy.

In September 2014 as part of the Climate Leadership in Action initiative, the World Bank launched a manifesto (officially called a statement) entitled "Putting a Price on Carbon" and, on 19 October 2015, World Bank Group President Jim Yong Kim and International Monetary Fund Managing Director Christine Lagarde launched "The Carbon Pricing Panel" with heads of government and supported by private sector leaders. "Carbon pricing", both initiatives make clear, is becoming the key to all strategies: there is no way around, thus it is claimed, putting a price on carbon in order to redirect investments on a scale close to the costs of climate change.

The manifesto has been signed by countries and corporations representing over 50 per cent of global gross national product; these include Germany, Deutsche Bank and Shell but not, for example, the USA and Australia. Nevertheless, the manifesto is rated as a breakthrough. Or, as the World Bank Vice-President responsible for climate issues, Rachel Kyte, put it at the 2014 Climate Conference in Lima: "It is no longer a question of if, but when and how." Hence, CO_2 pricing is becoming more and more of a key for defining climate policy as economic transformation in the context of Green Economy.

It should be noted that the debate around carbon pricing is a very confused one that mixes up quite a lot of different and very diverse approaches ranging from taxing upstream fossil fuel production (which can have some very positive effects) to carbon trading schemes. Yet, be this as it may, the example of the increasingly clear significance of "carbon pricing" as a silver-bullet strategy demonstrates that "monetisation" is not a bogey conjured up by paranoid critics of globalisation, but a real practice that is being driven forward by a powerful coalition of interests as a response to the global environmental and climate crisis — with fatal consequences.

Appropriation

Functions of nature, understood as natural capital, have the potential to become assets and hence tradable goods. Despite all the difficulties of creating functioning markets, in the case of CO_2 this has largely succeeded. But the object of CO_2 trading is naturally not the carbon dioxide itself, but certificates based on the juridical notion of pollution rights. Firms are allocated such pollution rights (as in the first phase of the European Union's emissions trading scheme), or else they have to buy them, normally at auction. Thus, tradable property rights in the form of certificates have been created. As a rule, this kind of trading is only made possible by setting upper limits, known as "caps", on CO_2 emissions. Only this capping creates a market and a demand; hence the name "cap and trade" for such trading systems.

The example shows that trade in such natural assets is linked to clearly defined property relations. As questionable as the construct of pollution rights may appear to many, it has proven effective for establishing trading between economic actors who are in a position to fulfil the complicated preconditions for it (establishment of a unit of measurement like the "carbon metric", legal form, etc.).

However, this changes radically if the reduction of assumed future CO_2 emissions from deforestation is incorporated into a CO_2 trade. For many years there have been discussions about including the emissions from deforestation within the framework of the UN climate negotiations under the abbreviation REDD (which stands for **Red**ucing Emissions from **D**eforestation and Forest **D**egradation) — a process that was formally finalised in the run-up to COP 21 in Paris. The Paris text recognises the need for adequate and predictable financial resources and other "positive incentives" for results-based payment approaches, which is the basis for the payment of environmental services (PES) such as forest conservation efforts. The Paris decision in its section on finance asks specifically for stronger efforts in co-ordinating such payment provisions, including via the Green Climate Fund (GCF). At the behest of Norway, the new fund is also asked to play a bigger role in results-based payment efforts. The crucial context of social and environmental safeguards, gender-responsiveness and benefit-sharing approaches that such PES schemes need to implement is referred to very much as an afterthought in the Paris outcome. For REDD, once again, the critical first step is to develop reliable methods for measuring the CO_2 released by deforestation. The task is not

The EU ETS – how does it work?

To limit the amount of greenhouse gas they churn out, various countries have set up emissions trading schemes as a key policy instrument. Via these cap and trade schemes, the legislator sets a limit (cap) on the total amount of greenhouse gas emissions permitted for a specific period in order to reduce these emissions in accordance with climate targets. Permits are allocated free of charge or auctioned (with one permit entitling the holder to emit, say, one tonne of CO_2). Companies required to participate in emissions trading must show that they have enough permits to cover their CO_2 emissions. The permits can be traded freely, with a price put on one tonne of CO_2. In all, 17 such schemes have been set up around the world, and several more are planned. The largest is the European Union Emissions Trading System (EU ETS), which is a transnational scheme. National schemes exist in New Zealand and South Korea; California, Tokyo and China have regional schemes. In 2016, some 6.8 billion tonnes of CO_2 equivalent will be covered by such measures. Emissions trading is based on two premises. First, it should limit emissions of the greenhouse gas CO_2 in a controllable manner. Second, the scheme aims to stimulate investment in mitigating climate change and make climate-friendly companies more competitive, thereby driving the much-needed decarbonisation of the economy. Sadly, for structural reasons, it does neither, as attested by how the European scheme has performed. Under heavy lobbying pressure, the EU set the permitted limits for emissions from 2008 far too generously and subsequently cut them back too slowly. From the start, the number of permits — termed "allowances" in the EU ETS — has been too high, so the prices they have attracted have been too low to stimulate investment in climate protection. In addition, governments have given away allowances for free to the most climate-damaging firms, handing them a big windfall. Between 2008 and 2012, the ten major beneficiaries made 3.2 billion euros by passing the cost of allowances through to their product prices and selling surplus allowances. The energy companies must now bid for the allowances they want, but lavish exemptions mean that nearly all polluters in the industry still get them for free. What's more, all companies continue to benefit from the transfer of their surplus allowances from earlier trading periods. The steel firm ArcelorMittal, for example, will not have to buy any extra allowances before 2024. In theory, emissions trading is capable of reducing CO_2 emissions. In practice, however, the trading system has not made a significant contribution to climate change mitigation. This is because of the "offset" credits that companies have been able to buy in large numbers outside the system since 2008 in order to meet their commitments. The reasoning goes like this: it does not matter where in the world the CO_2 emissions are cut, so rather than investing lots of money in reducing their own emissions, European companies may as well contribute to initiatives—such as the construction of a wind farm at lower cost—that save emissions elsewhere. The problem is that between one third and one half of such projects result in no additional benefit because the investments would have been made anyway. As a result, the climate impact of offset credits is not only close to zero, it is in some cases negative, due to the abuse of this mechanism. By the end of the second trading period in 2012, the number of additional allowances in Europe had risen to more than a billion as a result of the offsets, and during the third trading period, this figure could well increase to as much as 1.7 billion by 2020. By outsourcing reduction commitments, the offsets ease the pressure on industry to change its ways. Through offsets, oversupply, the economic crisis of 2008/9 and the associated erroneous forecasts, the number of excess allowances in Europe has risen to over two billion. As a result, the price of CO_2 is persistently far too low. Combined with low prices for coal and high prices for natural gas, coal has boomed in Europe. Between 2010 and 2013, emissions from this sector rose by six per cent because the price of CO_2 was not high enough to make power generated from the less harmful natural gas competitive with that of the more harmful coal. As a result, gas was squeezed out by coal. In a largely futile attempt at reform, the EU has agreed to withhold 900 million allowances for the time being (backloading). According to its most recent decision on reform, a market stability reserve will be introduced from 2019 in order to cushion the constant drop in prices; this operates by reducing the number of allowances being traded in the marketplace and placing them in reserve.

An alternative approach, used by several US states, as well as by Canada and Britain, is to impose CO_2 standards on power plants that use fossil fuel. Since 2013, the British government has set a minimum price for CO_2 and annual emission budgets for new power plants equivalent to the emissions from a modern gas-fired plant. Since 2014, France has charged a tax — albeit a small one — on fuels. The rate will quadruple until 2020. It is also possible to force old power plants offline by applying a technical criterion to their efficiency. The Netherlands will bring in a minimum requirement that will ensure that four older plants will shut down by 2017. Explicit criticism of emissions trading as the "wrong solution" came recently from an unexpected quarter. Pope Francis wrote in his encyclical "Laudato si" that emissions trading gives rise to a new type of speculation, yet does not serve the cause of cutting greenhouse gases. ■

Source: COAL ATLAS – Facts and figures on a fossil fuel (www.boell.de)

made simpler by the fact that CO_2 credits are not actually generated by deforestation but by the avoidance of deforestation. First it must be ascertained how much deforestation would normally be expected, and how much of a reduction is being achieved — in comparison to this hypothetical scenario — by targeted conservation measures. The resulting amount from the calculation can be converted into certificates. In this way, vague future forecasts (which are very susceptible to political manipulation) are being turned into financial market products.

Certification of the reduction of CO_2 emissions by projects was first developed in the context of the Clean Development Mechanism (CDM) under the Kyoto Protocol. Certified Emission Reduction (CER) is the name of the tradable and offsettable units which have been developed with considerable methodological effort.[80] Within the CDM, only projects for afforestation and reforestation qualify for carbon credits, not those for the reduction of deforestation. For such reduction, the Verified Carbon Standard (VCS) has been developed as the recognised standard. Although both the CDM and the REDD market are suffering from price slumps and insufficient demand, the essential set of instruments for the standardised measurement of CO_2 credits from (avoided) deforestation does exist and is in practical use. With the Paris Agreement these offset instruments are not dead. COP 21 established a whole new market mechanism for "sustainable development" to trade in "internationally transferred mitigation outcomes". And many countries have made it clear that they intend to achieve parts of their national climate targets through REDD approaches — either by implementing them or by providing funding as part of their international climate finance commitments. So despite the obvious failure of existing emission trading schemes to deliver a transformation away from fossil fuels, it is clear that some governments and many companies are not willing to let go of these flexibility mechanisms that allow for a greenwashed business as usual.

Based on the experience up until now, one trend is emerging ever more clearly: monetary valuation of the CO_2 storage in forests will not suffice, if the intention is to prevent the conversion of natural forest into land for intensive agricultural use, e.g. for soya production or palm oil plantations. Intensive use is more profitable. This is no longer disputed even by REDD supporters.[81]

Therefore the REDD mechanism is becoming increasingly uninteresting for large landowners and corporations, which are the main perpetrators of deforestation. Instead, indigenous peoples and local communities are observably becoming the primary target group of REDD projects, although they bear little of the responsibility for forest destruction. For them, the monetary incentives are likely to be sufficient to enable forest conservation measures, such as the prevention of forest clearance for shifting cultivation. Indigenous peoples and local communities are therefore set to become CO_2 traders. However, they cannot trade CO_2 like ceramics. An extensive system of calculations, reports and verification ("measurement, reporting and verification", MRV) is necessary, and CO_2 credits have to be certified. Communities thereby enter into dependency upon consulting firms and consultants who can fulfil these functions. And complicated questions about property rights must be resolved, because a new category of property rights comes into being: "carbon rights". Indigenous peoples and local communities see part of their habitat — the forest — being transformed by virtue of its CO_2 storage function into a (potentially) tradable product. Under the logic of the REDD mechanism, transfer payments to indigenous peoples are linked to verifiable outputs (CO_2 reduction); these are called "result based payments". Once they proceed down this road, the communities must submit to the rules of the market and adjust their way of life accordingly. Thus, at least to some extent, they lose control over their territory.

So far, this is all more of a scenario than a reality, but numerous conflicts in and around REDD projects indicate that the field of conflict outlined here is completely realistic.[82] Through mechanisms like REDD, large areas of the world that were previously managed by local communities can be swept into the vortex of CO_2 markets. The absurdity is that the very people who played the least part in global deforestation are now served by a market-compliant mechanism designed to prevent deforestation. This puts their life support base and their culture under simultaneous twin pressures: from the expansion of land for agricultural use in an industrialised farming system geared towards export, and from new, market-based mechanisms like REDD which are supposed to serve the conservation of forests and natural resources.

In the run-up to and at COP 21 in Paris debates on REDD focussed on a so-called "landscape approach" that aims at taking a look at the entire spectrum of "ecosystem services" provided by forests, plants and soils. REDD can thus be seen as a large-scale experiment in (progressively) integrating into the market territories, which were never previously subject to market logic and economic calculation. That path is conditioned by some fundamental assumptions of the Green Economy: that deforestation is caused by failing to value the ecosystem functions of the intact forest and by the lack of any economic incentive to conserve the forest — only now this economic logic is being applied to communities who have, actually, conserved the forest pretty well. Here is evidence that considering nature in such economic terms obstructs the view of the commons economy. Is it not the case that indigenous peoples and traditional communities have succeeded in conserving forests and ecosystems precisely by managing them as commons, as collective assets, embedded in community strategies and not subject to individual profit maximisation? Instead of strengthening the commons stewardship approach, instruments like REDD seek to establish a logic of valorisation that only makes sense if that value can be realised and property rights, in this case "carbon rights", are sold off.

More recent trends in the debate around climate, forests and agriculture enlarge upon the REDD approach and seek to develop complete landscape approaches, which take an all-encompassing overview of the CO_2 storage capacity and the ecosystem services of soils, trees and plants — throwing open the floodgates to a far more extensive loss of the rights and control traditionally exercised by the original inhabitants of these landscapes. Those rights and that control have until now provided local people with a life-support base and nature with a prospect of retaining its integrity.

Offsetting

The establishment of a carbon metric is indivisibly linked to the idea of equivalence. A tonne of CO_2 is a tonne of CO_2 — irrespective of where and how it arose. This is the logical consequence of an objectivised metric. CO_2 and its equivalents become tradable like petrol or potatoes. But if it is measurable and tradable, then it is also offsettable. Anyone who has a guilty conscience about taking a plane flight can compensate for the CO_2 emissions generated. For a flight from Berlin to New York, the asking price from the most reputable German supplier, atmosfair gGmbH, is 45 euros. This money is then used to support climate-friendly projects aimed at cancelling out the emissions from the flight. The emissions from that particular flight might be offset by a forest project in Latin America, for example. The sheer variety of offsetting schemes on offer is increasingly bringing this idea into everyday circulation; it is being normalised.

Carbon offsetting is one of the key concepts of international climate policy. Two of the Kyoto Protocol mechanisms, the Clean Development Mechanism (CDM) and Joint Implementation (JI), are designed as offsetting mechanisms. Offsets from both of these mechanisms can be used — with certain restrictions — in European emissions trading.[83] As described above, the Paris Climate Change Conference opened the door for a new era of offsetting through a new market mechanism that will most likely include REDD.

Despite the above-mentioned difficulty of CO_2 trading at the present time, offsetting is an established practice with existing and recognised units of measure. There is controversy over the extent to which REDD should function as an offset mechanism; a powerful coalition of interests exists which wants this, but there is also serious opposition.

Interventions other than forest conservation can also be recorded, quantified, standardised and traded. Some of the examples are surprising. For example, in the context of Californian emissions trading, provision is made for offsets from rice farming: "The proposed 'Compliance Offset Protocol Rice Cultivation Projects' would allow rice farmers in the Sacramento Valley to generate greenhouse gas offsets that can then be sold on the state's carbon trading market. Rice would represent the first crop-based agricultural offset protocol, paving the way for additional agriculture-based protocols to be developed."[84]

Behind the idea of offsetting is the ultimate aim of achieving a "net reduction" of CO_2 emissions or "net zero emissions" in the long-term: "In a year's time, the international community will have the opportunity to send a clear signal that we, as a global community, are determined to manage our economies to achieve zero net emissions before the year 2100" — to quote the World Bank Group President Jim Yong King.[85]

The rationale behind the net zero emissions idea is that the world can keep producing emissions as long as there is a way to "balance them out" by offsetting. So, instead of commencing radical emissions reduction immediately, we should continue to be able to emit vast quantities of CO_2 — and even construct new coal-fired power plants — whilst claiming to be engaging in climate change mitigation by advancing the development of CO_2 storage technologies.[86]

Not only can CO_2 storage propel us into the world of net zero emissions, but by creating more sinks, for instance by planting trees, emissions may even be overcompensated. This gives rise to "negative emissions", which can offset emissions in other places. Politically speaking, such constructs have already become eminently important and influential.

It is astounding to witness the popularisation of a new notion of nature by means of a catchy phrase like "net zero", as it becomes ingrained in everyday usage. While contentious terms such as "climate neutrality", "net zero emissions" or "decarbonisation" (which all have significantly different meanings) did not make it into the Paris Agreement, the compromise was to resort to IPCC language, with the final text calling for a *peaking* of greenhouse gas emissions as soon as possible "so as to achieve a balance of anthropogenic emissions by sources and removals by sinks of greenhouse gases in the second half of this century," which many observers understand to equal a "net zero" approach.

All of this sheds light on where framing the issue with the concept of "natural capital" is leading: elements of nature are interchangeable and offsettable. In climate policy, the net-zero approach brings nature and economics together in one big offsetting scheme, or in the words of the World Bank Vice-President, Rachel Kyte: "The latest report from the Intergovernmental Panel on Climate Change (IPCC) tells us that to rein in climate change and keep global warming under 2 °C, we will have to start reducing emissions now and get to near net zero emissions within this century. We've known for a long time that slowing deforestation and planting forests can slow CO_2 emissions and nature's CO_2 storage capacity can help us get to net zero emissions, and that investment in climate-smart land-use can increase that storage […]."[87]

So land use becomes a key question in climate policy and vice versa.[88] We will come back to this point later when we discuss geoengineering as a key technology envisaged to create "negative emissions".

Biodiversity loss –
quantifying, appropriating, offsetting

Seeing nature as a provider of ecosystem services is an idea that has skyrocketed in popularity in recent years. Describing nature as a service provider changes the perception of nature, and this is entirely intentional. The terminology was introduced in order to protect nature and to make it clear that humans are wholly dependent upon nature. Human well-being depends on an intact natural world — that was the central message of the Millennium Ecosystem Assessment (MA), which contributed substantially to the popularisation of the "ecosystem services" concept in 2003. For all too often, economics notices only the direct exploitation of nature: it recognises the forest as a wood supplier but not an ecosystem that has many other functions, such as keeping the air clean, storing CO_2 or providing clean water through filtration. The ecosystem approach aims to bring this into focus, but sheer visibility is only half the battle, as exemplified by a publication of the German Federal Ministry for Economic Cooperation and Development (BMZ) that states: "Nature makes a multitude of services and resources available to humankind. For example, these include clean water, healthy soils, protection from flooding and soil erosion, medicines, carbon storage, climate regulation and recreation. Although humankind is dependent on these services of nature, no prices or markets for them exist. They are barely perceived as an economic asset, and for a long time their value was estimated to be minimal."[89]

Spurred on by the resounding publicity garnered by the Stern Report, in the year 2007 under the leadership of Pavan Sukhdev an initiative for the economic assessment of ecosystems was finally brought into being, The Economics of Ecosystems and Biodiversity (TEEB). The aim is to tie nature conservation into an economic rationale.

TEEB ventures onto substantially more difficult terrain than Stern. The economic valuation of nature is complicated and controversial — the studies published by TEEB do not deny that. Even though TEEB was unable to reach a consensus, the project did contribute to popularising the concept of "natural capital" and to inculcating an economic view of nature into more and more political discourses. For instance, the EU now has a "workstream" for "Natural Capital Accounting" and a "Natural Capital Financing Facility".

For the advocates of such an economic approach, rendering the services of nature visible is not their only concern by far: "In order to apportion more equitably the costs arising for the preservation of ecosystems, various mechanisms have been developed in past years. One of the established methods is 'payments for ecosystem services' (PES). This is underpinned by the idea that those who contribute to the conservation of ecosystems — the local population, often indigenous communities — should be paid for this by the beneficiaries of the ecosystem service."[90]

Initially, this is a persuasive idea, because ultimately human well-being depends on the functions of nature, yet it is mixed up with a problematic diagnosis of causes: the absence of prices and markets is assumed to be the root of all evil. The recognition of ecosystem services results in the plausible requirement for payment for ecosys-

Payment for environmental services – a typology

The term "payment for ecosystem services" (PES) is applied to many different types of payment scheme:

- PES using public funding—in other words, subsidies—to protect ecosystems, such as the EU paying farmers to preserve biodiversity under the Common Agricultural Policy
- Payments by companies or entities to improve their image ("greenwashing")
- Voluntary payments to offset pollution or the destruction of nature
- PES as permission to destroy or pollute above a legal limit.[91] ■

tem services (PES) as a logical conclusion. The link with the Green Economy idea is evident: no prices and markets exist for the services of nature; therefore, prices must be determined and markets created. PES is often dealt with in the context of what are known as market-based instruments (MBI), one of the great beacons of hope of international environmental policy. The reasons for their popularity are only too obvious: market-based instruments take the pressure off the state, no new costs are incurred for environmental policy, and implementation is flexible, being negotiated between market participants.

PES projects and framework legislation have sprung up in many countries around the world. Mexico and Costa Rica are considered the leading nations. The lion's share of PES projects is found in the water sector. For example, a regional water corporation pays landowners to desist from certain agricultural practices (such as the use of nitrogenous fertilisers), and hence to contribute to the provision of clean drinking water.

The consequences for the given population living in the ecosystems to be protected are as diverse in these different types of PES as the advantages that polluters can derive from them. Therefore a debate has evolved around PES; this, together with evaluations of PES approaches, permits some initial conclusions:

- The usage of the term PES is extremely vague and encompasses very different approaches.[92]

- Many PES projects are not market-based instruments but are more akin to classic and familiar environmental subsidies. A study about PES in Costa Rica therefore talks about "subsidies in disguise".[93]

- The overwhelming majority of all PES projects (over 90 per cent) are financed with public money.[94]

- While such subsidies do include transfer payments, these are not based on putting a value on nature's "services".

- Most PES projects, then, are not remunerating nature's services but are influencing certain forms of human management of nature by means of monetary incentives.

Perhaps the greatest innovation under PES is not the practice but the language, the wording. Under the ecosystem services approach, or PES, nature is described in economic terms, creating and inculcating the logical basis for monetisation and market-based instruments.[95] The previous lack of prices and the necessity of creating markets becomes a mantra for politico-economic discourses — regardless of the fact that, as already mentioned, these often only disguise conventional subsidies from public funds.

For a rigorous further development of the PES approach, the monetary valuation of ecosystem services is likewise essential. Even the proponents of the ecosystem approach admit — to varying degrees — that far from all of nature's services can be accounted for in monetary terms; yet in order to establish new market instruments or payment systems, they consider monetary valuation to be indispensable even if they frankly concede that it falls short of perfection. Complex ecosystem functions are hard to assess, given that there are great

Biodiversity offsets –
the example of Gabon

On 1 August 2014, the small Central African country of Gabon adopted a Sustainable Development Law (SDL), which introduces a social and environmental offsetting system. Until now, the global trend towards more flexible environmental legislation has focused mainly on the introduction of market mechanisms (e.g. biodiversity offsets) as a way of compensating for the destruction of nature. Gabon has now taken this approach a step further by extending it to local communities' rights as well, which means that violations of rights resulting from the exploitation of natural resources can now be offset. The British NGO Fern and the Gabon-based NGO Brainforest have analysed the new law.[96] In essence, the SDL is a "framework law", meaning that details will be elaborated in future legislation. This will be done with the aid of a group of European consultants, including representatives of Ecocert, Adetef and Carbone 4, funded by the European Commission. The Sustainable Development Law of Gabon, which the international law firm Baker & McKenzie helped to write, establishes a national market for various types of credit: carbon credits, biodiversity credits, ecosystem credits, and community capital credits, the latter defined as the "sum of the natural and cultural assets belonging to a community". Under the SDL, credits can be generated during the course of a development project by reducing CO_2 emissions, by preserving an area of biodiversity, or creating a certain number of jobs, for example. An annual national sustainable development survey will calculate the total level of sustainable development assets, which is equal to the sum of all biodiversity, community, carbon and ecosystem credits. These credits will all be recorded in an inventory, known as the national sustainable development register. This is essential for trading to take place. The system will allow full exchangeability across all credit types, meaning, for example, that CO_2 emissions from a project in one area can be offset by building a school for a community in another, and vice versa. The system not only poses serious problems with measurement and implementation, it also violates international law. Gabon has signed numerous international human rights conventions. The offsetting system undermines local communities' fundamental rights of access to their natural resources and culture. Gabon is a resource-rich country; among other things, it has substantial iron ore deposits, such as the Belinga iron reserves, which are among the largest in the world. The government plans to launch a formal licence tender in 2016. Many international mining companies and resource-dependent countries (such as China) have their eye on this wealth although their hunger is currently slightly abated by a decrease in global commodity prices. An offsetting system for the damage to human health and the natural environment caused by resource extraction would play right into their hands. After all, it is much easier to write a cheque than to comply with national and international law.[97] ∎

uncertainties and that regional contexts exert their own influence. The provision of clean air is a different challenge in Guangzhou than in Alaska. Despite the exuberance of the economic language: markets for ecosystem services either do not exist, or are regionally limited, like "habitat banking", for example. The only hope for a global PES mechanism is the above-mentioned REDD (Reducing Emissions from Deforestation and Forest Degradation), i.e. the much discussed idea that the worldwide conservation of forests as carbon sinks is to be financed by all. Yet, as has been shown, this is another mechanism that ultimately revolves around CO_2.

Here once again—as in the climate debate—the offsetting described above is of central significance to the debate about the economisation of ecosystem services. The destruction of biodiversity, i.e. nature, is to be compensated by means of "biodiversity offsetting". Biodiversity markets already exist; probably the most important is US Wetland Banking. If wetlands are destroyed by a construction project, for instance, the building contractor, instead of financing direct mitigation measures, can buy offsets which have been generated by restoring, conserving or creating wetlands elsewhere. Wetlands have a price which depends on local factors. Wetland Banking turns over around one to two billion US dollars per year. The goal is "no net loss", meaning that losses in one location should be equalised by conservation measures in another in order to arrive at "net zero". The parallels with the climate debate are neither accidental not unintentional, but the result of transference of political approaches and instruments — albeit without having reflected on their effectiveness.

For offsetting, units of measure are a requirement: "Biodiversity currencies, like financial currencies, are designed to facilitate trade and exchange. This means they must be fungible, i.e. allow exchange using a common unit of loss and gain. Governments, Rio Tinto and BBOP projects[98] regularly use Extent x Condition currencies […]. These currencies are a multiplication of quantity and quality."[99]

"Fungibility", meaning the easy substitutability of goods, is the keyword here. The above quote originates not from critics but from users of existing biodiversity offsets. It is not by chance that their ranks include some of the major global mining corporations, in particular. Offsetting allows them to carry out their activities at a bearable price. Offsetting is a mechanism which facilitates rather than constrains. A price has to be paid for this facilitation, so that in the end everything is deemed to be evened out — "no net loss".

This idea of compensation, which is rooted in the practice of biodiversity offsetting, is increasingly becoming a central reference point of integrative policy approaches. (The "no net loss" approach starts from the assumption — as already outlined — that biodiversity loss in one place can be compensated by conservation or promotion of biodiversity somewhere else.) In the context of its Biodiversity Strategy 2020 the EU is considering possible new legislation on biodiver-

The wonders of offsetting: green uranium

Namibia has immensely rich and diverse ecosystems—but it also has vast uranium deposits beneath them. This is not a problem, apparently, because now, there is "green uranium", whose extraction will have positive environmental impacts. At least, that is what mine operators and Flora & Fauna International (FFI), one of the world's oldest environmental organisations, are claiming. Biodiversity offsets are the key. "Fortunately, the mining companies in the area welcome this concept. Rössing Uranium Ltd is committed, under its corporate mandate of Rio Tinto, to achieve a net positive impact on biodiversity."[100] The Rössing uranium mine is one of the largest in the world, with Rio Tinto—one of the largest global mining companies— holding a 69 per cent stake in it. Biodiversity offsets are obviously intended to legitimise uranium extraction here and ease its way towards political acceptance. After all, a mine with a supposedly positive impact on the biodiversity balance sheet is much easier to "sell". Environmental organisations' increasing tendency to partner with companies engaged in mining operations is a major issue, but also a sensitive one, in the brave new world of offset-based environmental protection. Of course, it is clear that offsets are necessary and useful when such projects simply cannot be avoided. However, they also facilitate and greenwash projects that raise justifiable concerns, which is why critical environmental organisations call them "a licence to trash".[101] ■

sity offsets (called the "No Net Loss" initiative) which could cancel out existing environmental directives. The objective would be "no net loss of biodiversity"—an important difference from the previous goal of "no loss".[102]

The valorisation of ecosystem services, monetary valuation of such services and the creation of trading systems for the purpose of compensating for the degradation of nature essentially follow the approaches seen as successful in climate policy. Methodologically, the monetary valuation of ecosystem services outside of the CO_2 debate is still lagging badly behind. But that does not prevent those who profit from compensation options, such as the large mining corporations, from forcing the pace of further development and implementation. The questions that arise concerning property rights, resource equity and socio-environmental justice are self-evident.

As outlined, in the context of a new valuation of nature, numerous mechanisms for accounting and offsetting have been created. What is fundamental is that functions of nature like the storage of CO_2 by trees can be offset against human-induced environmental degradation. Quantification has brought nature and human activities down to a common denominator. But of course, it is not nature that is captured in this offsetting mode, it is quantifiable nature, a very specific construct of nature, whereby only what is countable is deemed really to count. Some more recently developed approaches make the assumption of fungibility, i.e. exchangability and tradability, not just of ecosystem functions in different regions or hemispheres or between different functions — for example, CO_2 storage capacity versus provision of fresh air — but also see potential for compensating between ecological and social harms. Such approaches may be seen as exceptions for the time being. However, the multifaceted practice of economisation of nature in climate policy makes it clear that we have long ventured onto a slippery slope and are starting to slide. The red lines — emergency brakes and alternatives — can only be defined by politics, not the market, and that requires a re-politicisation of environmental policy.

7

Progress in the service of the Green Economy: will innovation solve everything?

In every transformation strategy and in all the Green Economy conceptions, technological innovations take on a pivotal role. All eyes look to them to increase resource productivity and replace scarce resources. Innovations generate new growth and thus deliver on Green Economy's promise — green growth becomes a possibility.

We undoubtedly need innovations! Without new ideas and inventions we are marching on the spot and will not master the complex challenges of the future.

But the question is, how can we convert our entire energy base to renewables, intelligently and efficiently, without either provoking new environmental and social crises or upholding our own lifestyles and patterns of production at the cost of people and the natural environment in other countries? Moreover, how can we make the leap into a "zero waste" economy? Which production methods will best equip smallholders in the tropics to cope with the uncertainties caused by climate change? Which rules do we need in order to turn a profit-maximising economy into one that is geared towards human needs, sharing and justice?

All these are questions that are not, as yet, attracting anywhere near sufficient resources — be they conceptual, financial or human. Such questions could be conducive to a whole new wave of innovations which would make our economy and society sustainable, more equitable and "fit for our grandchildren".

Unfortunately the innovation debate within the Green Economy mainstream is pursuing rather a one-track approach, determined exclusively by economic parameters and vested interests. Often those who lay claim to being particularly innovative are the very ones who ensure that socially equitable and long-term environmental solutions are marginalised. This emerges especially clearly, for example, when it comes to the question of seeds. An abundance of seeds — combined with an abundance of collective and locality-specific (historical) knowledge about production methods — promises a great deal more innovativeness and locally-applicable solutions than a seed market dominated and patented by a handful of multinational corporations in which, for example, 45 per cent of private seed-related research funding is being invested in a single species, namely maize.[103]

"Innovation" has become a key concept and has evidently taken over from "progress" as the main idea informing economic and political action. If the Great Transformation is to succeed, innovation is a decisive factor, without a doubt. But many of Green Economy's protagonists trust almost blindly in technological innovation. Nowhere near as much attention is paid to cultural and social innovations — be they new ideas or ancient ones revived. The greatest hope is vested in the resource and efficiency revolution driven by new technologies. In particular, these are expected to accomplish the decoupling of gross domestic product (GDP) from resource consumption.

Innovations — as imperative as they are — always need to be considered in their social and environmental settings. The consequences of new technologies for people and the environment are not always meticulously surveyed, however, and are far too little debated in the political and democratic process. In the case of technologies like geo-engineering or synthetic biology (both of which will be discussed below), the environmental, social and economic consequences are simply not foreseeable. Therefore, it is vital to look carefully at why and for whom innovations are being developed and who ultimately profits from them (and from the belief in them).

An additional aspect comes into play: "To talk about 'innovation' seems to free us from the ideological ballast of 'progress' and demands no presumption of a judgement about whether the new is actually good or bad. For the 'innovation' fetish, simply everything that is new is good. 'Innovation' often appears to be devoid of content, but is not free of ideology."[104]

Innovation is repeatedly linked with the promise of growth. Thus, in its 2020 strategy, the European Union defines itself as an "Innovation Union", linking that notion to three objectives: intelligent growth, sustainable growth and integrative growth.[105]

The Green Economy version of this is to be found in the New Climate Economy Report: "Innovation is central to economic growth, as long-term trends in productivity and growth are largely determined by trends in innovation. [...] it is essential to transforming global energy systems, agriculture and cities — every aspect of the economy. [...] Innovation also makes it possible to continue growing our economies in a world of finite resources."[106]

The question is not whether "we" or society are for or against technology or innovations. Nobody wishes themselves back in the days when operations were carried out without anaesthetic. Only in the second half of the 19th century did anaesthesia come into common use following the "discovery" of ether as an anaesthetic. In the growth-centred approaches of Green Economy, however, the issue is not individual innovations and their value, but innovation as a principle and as a saviour. These become the necessary conditions for green growth to function at all.

To speak about innovation and technological progress is to speak about the future, and this, as we know, tends to be uncharted territory. This makes it all the more remarkable to see innovation held up as a cure-all with such absolute confidence. In the last three centuries we have undoubtedly witnessed a far-reaching revolution associated with fundamental innovations. It has rightly been commented that if a Roman from the era around the birth of Christ were transported to early 18th-century London, he would have found himself in somewhat strange but not completely unfamiliar surroundings. In particular, transport continued to be based on human and horse power. 300 years later, however, the ancient Roman would have encountered a completely different environment. Electric lighting, subway systems, cars, concrete, computers, mobile phones — all these are innovations of the last 300 years.

The industrial revolution is primarily an energy revolution; it has fundamentally altered the metabolism between society and nature. Jason Moore describes capitalism as a way of organising nature: "The mosaic of human activity in the web of life is reduced to an abstract humanity as homogenous acting unit. Inequality, commodification, imperialism, patriarchy, and much more. At best, these relations are acknowledged, but as after-the-fact supplements to the framing of the problem. This framing unfolds from an eminently commonsensical, yet I think also profoundly misleading, narrative: one in which the 'human enterprise' is set against the 'great forces of nature'. [...] This is the 'One System/Two Systems' problem common to green thought in its mainstream and critical currents."[107] While Jason Moore rightly traces the origins of the "Capitalocene" back to the 16th century and the colonial times, only the massive use of fossil energy enabled the rapid developments of the modern era and laid the foundation for a growth dynamic unparalleled in human history. The modern era can rightly be called the "fossil fuels regime". The decisive breakthrough was the extraction of coal by means of steam pumps. The use of coal in mining enabled the extraction of more and more coal, and ultimately oil deposits could also be exploited. The economy and population are growing rapidly on the basis of an energy regime which, within the briefest window of time, has accessed and exploited fossil deposits in the form of coal, oil and gas built up over millions of years.

Taking leave of this model is no less than a complete departure from the basis of development for the last three centuries.[108]

The extraction of fossil fuels, in turn, is associated with the worldwide exploitation of metal and mineral resources. On the basis of the large volumes of energy available, natural resources become the material foundation of development. Steel and cement play a prominent role in this. Looking at development over recent centuries, it would therefore be a mistake only to look at energy generation. In order to deliver on the promise of "growth in a world of finite resources", not only must the energy base of our civilisation be overhauled but the consumption of materials must also change radically. Therefore, alongside 100 per cent renewable energies—and hence *decarbonisation*—the second key concept for the path to a Green Economy is *dematerialisation*.

Subsumed under the neat heading of "innovation" are very different and varied developments. These will be elucidated with examples below, and in this way we can avoid drifting into a general and futile debate along the lines of "innovation—blessing or curse". Humankind develops and adapts its modes of production. To begin with, this is a simple fact, but a more precise balance-sheet analysis of a few developments may help to provide a clearer assessment of the potentials and limitations of innovation.

The materials of the world as we know it: steel and cement

Amidst all the chatter about new technologies (IT and digitalisation), steel and cement are almost dinosaurs of the modern era, not in the sense of extinct, but more like chipper veterans of the fossil age. Common to both: their production is energy-intensive; therefore massive-scale use of them only became possible in the age of cheap fossil energy. Steel and cement are not sexy and rarely step into the spotlight of public interest, but precisely for that reason these two materials are highly instructive to look at. Powerful industries have invested a great deal in innovation in recent decades in order to come up with more environmentally friendly production processes for both materials.

Cement and concrete (which consists of one-third cement) are the most important man-made materials of the modern era by some margin. In the year 2012, four billion tonnes of cement were produced. China accounts for 58 per cent of global production, but India (with a seven per cent share) also produces more than Europe. In 2001, production in China was only 595 million tonnes. While air pollution with cement is largely controllable with modern filters, cement pro-

Green steel = green sheen

Sensing which way the wind is blowing, the steel industry is looking for ways to greenwash its notoriously dirty production system. In partnership with the federal government in Brazil, it is replacing coal with biomass charcoal in its smelting operations. According to industry calculations, producing one tonne of pig iron emits 1.9 tonnes of CO_2, while "green steel" removes 1.1 tonnes of gas from the atmosphere. How does it work? Well, the truth is that it doesn't. It's a classic example of greenwashing — with support from UNEP, among others. The charcoal is derived from fast growing eucalyptus from plantations already owned and managed by the steel companies. Using charcoal saves them money as it is far cheaper than buying coke on the world markets. What's more, by replacing coke with charcoal, the companies are hoping to earn carbon credits, which they can then sell. The EU is jumping on the bandwagon as well, with UCLOS, which stands for Ultra Low Carbon Dioxide Steelmaking — a consortium of 48 corporate and institutional partners from 15 European countries, including all the major EU steel companies and various research institutes and universities, set up with the European Commission's support. The ULCOS research programme focuses mainly on the use of biomass and CCS technology.[109] But "green steel" is a classic example of "green sheen". It fails to take into account that trees take a long time to regenerate and store the carbon dioxide emissions from charcoal burning. Making matters worse, coal is biomass energy that has become densely concentrated over millions of years, so more biomass than coal is needed to produce the same amount of power. Eucalyptus is not native to Brazil and causes a high level of soil acidification. In Brazil, this type of monoculture is often associated not only with a high loss of biodiversity and soil fertility but also with clearing of land, poor working

conditions and expulsion of local communities. The fact that
UNEP is describing "green steel" charcoal as a "greenhouse neutral" energy source is an absolute scandal.[110] ∎

duction remains one of the largest emitters of CO_2. Efficiency gains
have not kept pace relative to the growth in production. Whereas in
1950 cement production accounted for just a one per cent share of the
global emissions from fossil fuel combustion, in 2010 it was almost
five per cent.[111]

A similar trend is seen with steel: China is responsible for half of
global steel production. It produces far more than the EU and the
USA combined. In 1990, Chinese production was still only 66 million
tonnes, but had risen to more than 800 million tonnes in 2015 (albeit
down by 2.3 per cent on 2014). By way of comparison: the EU produced around 166 million tonnes in 2015 and the USA around 79 million tonnes.[112]

The growth of cement and steel production has accelerated in the
last 20 years, i.e. during a period in which climate and environmental problems were already clearly identified and the search for new
technological solutions was at full tilt. The "classic" man-made materials of the fossil age have not in any way been replaced by new wonder materials. Now, as ever, cement and steel are the basis of human
development in the modern era. So far, no trend towards dematerialisation is in sight for the world's mainstay materials. Undoubtedly,
new technologies are diminishing the energy-intensity in the production of these materials, yet industry itself is not unduly optimis-
tic regarding the potential for reining in CO_2 emissions: "Global CO_2
emissions of ThyssenKrupp are mostly influenced by the production
figures of steel. The steel production accounts for more than 90 per
cent of emissions. Already applying the most advanced technologies
major reductions are not to be achieved. The increase of CO_2 emissions from 2011/2012 until 2013/2014 is primarily related to a higher
steel production."[113]

World crude steel production 2014 and 2015 (in million tonnes Mt)

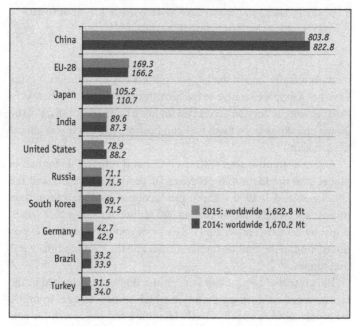

Source: World Steel Association

Despite this, steel and cement production have become cleaner and more efficient in recent years. They are growing inexorably, however, and consuming more and more energy. No miracle of innovation has managed to change that. So it comes as no surprise that the steel industry at EU level as well as in Germany is pulling financial and political levers in a lobbying campaign to undermine the Feed-In-Tariff Law (Erneuerbare-Energien-Gesetz, EEG) in order to secure continuing access to cheap coal-generated electricity and to exemptions in the electricity market. One example of such lobbying is the Initiative New Social Market Economy (INSM) financed by Gesamtmetall (Federation of German Employers' Associations in the Metal and Electrical Engineering Industries).

The motor car –
lessons on innovation, power and culture

The automobile industry is a key industry for the modern era; the famous Ford Model T is virtually a symbol of industrial society. The rise of the motor car as a mass-ownership vehicle and consumer product is directly linked to the history of oil. Only the fact that oil is a readily available and relatively low-cost energy source makes the car affordable to broader sections of the population. Virtually no single product can have stamped its mark on today's infrastructure as strongly as the car.

The pre-eminent importance of the automobile industry is a global phenomenon that withstood the crisis of 2008 without ill effects. In 2014, the worldwide number of newly registered private cars reached a new record high of 76 million. And the United States automobile industry defied its rumoured death to make a marvellous recovery: in 2014, more private cars were registered in the USA (16.4 million) than in the whole of Europe. Of course, the most important car market is now China, which holds the number one position in the world with 18.4 million new registrations. But even in a country like Brazil, a so-called emerging economy, the car industry is considered to be the prime driver of industrial production. In 2014, despite the crisis and a contraction in production, more motor cars were sold in Brazil (3.3 million) than in the whole of Eastern Europe (3.1 million).[114]

Today, the automobile industry is the most important branch of Germany's industrial base. It is the branch that managed to evade the "de-industrialisation" of recent decades. Today, Germany is much more of a car nation than twenty years ago. The figures are imposing: every year, billions are sunk into research for the ongoing advancement of the automobile.

"Das Auto" (The Car)—in the simple, succinct words used by Volkswagen (VW) to advertise its product, even in non-German-speaking countries—is also a symbol for the productivity and innovative spirit of Germany's industrial base. BMW, Mercedes, Audi and

"The Car" – a scandal
as an object lesson in Green Economy

"Volkswagen pursues a systematic CO_2 avoidance strategy and is on track to become a trailblazer for the Green Economy"— such was the praise heaped on the corporation in 2013 by the then German environment minister, Peter Altmaier.

The latest series of scandals in the car industry not only sheds light on the business practices of automobile corporations but also raises the question of what their commitments to Green Economy are really worth. For, so we are told, Green Economy was never intended to be a marketing concept or a PR strategy, but a new economic paradigm that responds to global challenges.

In October 2014, following investigations by the US environmental authorities, the Volkswagen Group had no choice but to concede that its tests to determine diesel engine emissions were falsified by using special software. 11 million cars, from Volkswagen Group alone, are affected. This manipulation not only distorted the vehicles' CO_2 readings but also the nitrous oxide emissions, which are considered especially harmful to health. This scandal has to do with climate policy. In particular, German and to a lesser extent French firms invested in diesel engines so as to comply with EU limits for CO_2 emissions.

"Diesel technology makes a valuable contribution by saving CO_2, enabling us to achieve our climate targets" explained the German Minister of Transport, Alexander Dobrindt.

The emissions scandal thus becomes a woeful object lesson of Green Economy: to achieve short-term CO_2 targets, a powerful and supposedly highly innovative industry invested in a technological path that enables it to perpetuate its old business model—despite considerable pollution of the environment. In France, two-thirds of all new cars run on diesel engines, and in

Paris, the city of the climate agreement, the consequences have meanwhile become so drastic that the mayor is demanding a general ban on diesel vehicles.

The two most important European car countries have blundered into a fatal dependency upon diesel and, using the argument of low CO_2 emissions, have insisted on pursuing a health-impairing technology that can ultimately have no future.

Now, anyone who believed that the most recent scandals might, at long last, precipitate a fundamental change of course witnessed instead an impressive demonstration of the lobbying prowess of the European car corporations. It had long been realised that test procedures conducted under unrealistic conditions yield emissions values significantly lower than those measured in everyday use. Now, moves are finally afoot within the European Parliament to agree a new, realistic test procedure called "real driving emissions" (RDE). This was passed on 3 February 2016, however not before the regulations had been softened in the interim to the point that the car industry was satisfied. Effectively, until 2021, car manufacturers are permitted to exceed, by more than double, the current threshold specified in the EURO 6 standard for nitrogen oxides. And even after this date it will still be permissible to exceed the limit values markedly. This approach by the EU meant making "the principle of exceeding threshold values into law", commented the Green Member of the European Parliament, Rebecca Harms. Corporate Europe Observatory dubbed the law the "loophole of all loopholes" and documented in detail the lobbying efforts of the European car industry that led to this outcome.[115]

The "VW scandal" has long been on the agenda of global political discourse, and other car corporations are no angels, either. Barely any other sector is such a fertile source for studying the closely interwoven nature of political and economic interests — in Germany and beyond. ▪

The German automotive industry: key figures (2013)

Sales	362 billion euros
Automotive sales as a per cent of total industry turnover	22 per cent (1991: 12.5 per cent)
Employees	756,000 (2014: 785,000)
Automotive share of total industrial workforce	14 per cent (1991: 9 per cent)
Jobs directly or indirectly connected to the automotive industry	approx. 5 million
Automotive industry share of trade surplus / total trade surplus	120 billion euros / 198 billion euros
Contribution to total tax revenue	around 25 per cent
Gross capital investment / internal R&D expenditure	14.4 billion euros / 18.3 billion euros
Share of total industrial investment / R&D	26 per cent / 33 per cent

Source: VDA

Porsche stand for the most modern technologies and refinements in the global automobile market.

The motor car's status as a key to modern industrial production makes it an eminently suitable case study of the achievements and limitations of innovation.[116] With an eye to the future, however, the question that remains to be addressed is: how prepared is the automobile industry for decarbonisation, for dematerialisation, for a low-CO_2 and resource-efficient future?

There is no denying that transport is one of the decisive sources of global CO_2 emissions — and that the trend is troubling indeed: "Over the past decade, transport's GHG emissions have increased at a faster rate than any other energy using sector (high agreement, much evidence)" — the IPCC reports.[117]

Transport accounts for the second-largest share of German CO_2 emissions after the energy industry.[118] The figure of 20 per cent exceeds those for the processing industry and for households. More than half of all transport-related emissions are attributable to individual private transport. And no other sector has so far contributed so little to emissions reduction as transport. Emissions from private vehicles fell by only five per cent,[119] and total transport emissions declined by only six per cent between 1990 and 2010, primarily due to increases in the emissions from transport of goods and aviation. For comparison: processing industries achieved a reduction of 35 per cent. Cars have, of course, become more fuel efficient but despite that, the bottom line figure is not very impressive. Between 2001 and 2010, a motor car's average fuel consumption dropped from 8.5 to 7.9 litres of petrol and from 6.9 to 6.6 litres of diesel — definitely no miracle of innovation. If we consider only the emissions of new cars, the balance sheet looks somewhat better, because in this category CO_2 emissions fell between the years 2003 and 2014 (first half-year) from 175 grammes per kilometre to 134.[120]

There is a reason for the poor overall result: although engines are becoming more and more fuel efficient due to innovation, this effect is partially cancelled out by increasingly powerful and heavier cars. In the year 2000, heavy SUVs only accounted for 2.9 per cent of new registrations; by 2014 this had risen to 17.9 per cent, and the car industry expects this trend to continue.

In 2014, the average engine power of a newly registered car in Germany was 140 HP, an increase of 47 per cent in the last 20 years.[121]

Furthermore, cars are becoming heavier by the year — requiring the consumption of ever more material. Nowadays, the average new car in Germany weighs 1,484 kilograms. Today, the Germans' most popular car, the VW Golf, weighs over 1,200 kilograms; the original model weighed 750. The trend can be observed worldwide: in the USA, a car weighs around 1,850 kilograms on average; at the beginning of the car boom in the year 1920, the average was only 540 kilogrammes.[122]

Alternative drive systems which were supposed to solve all energy problems have remained an empty promise. Almost all cars run on diesel or petrol, the same as ever. Yet the balance-sheet could look quite different. Lighter and more fuel efficient cars are not a technical challenge and are readily available. Likewise, the gas-driven vehicles on offer are tried and tested; their carbon footprint is distinctly better but they carve out a niche existence. More and more people want heavy, powerful cars — despite climate change.

When it comes to choosing a car, then, neither *homo oeconomicus* nor the environmentally informed consumer are the dominant influences on many people's thinking. Cars are obviously a central component of a "culture". Choices are influenced by cultural models. SUVs are appealing, they reflect a masculine ideal, they pay homage to a culture of strength, and they underscore hierarchies in road traffic. While the proportion of women among SUV buyers has risen to over 20 per cent, the most popular cars for women are small cars like the VW Up and the Twingo.[123]

Cars are a means of transport — but they are more than that. This is not an attempt to shift the "blame" — as the car industry does repeatedly — onto consumers, because they, after all, demand SUVs and cars with beefed-up engine power. It is the automobile industry that manufactures them and produces or promotes the mental images which take shape in SUVs and sporty "gas-guzzlers". What is more, the car industry keep dispatching its lobbyists to delay and tone down reduction targets for fuels — usually with success, as in the case of the law to introduce an efficiency label, which the industry largely wrote itself.[124] Most of all, they are keen on close contact with policymakers up to the highest level.[125] They have always made the self-defined competitiveness of the German automobile industry and Germany's strengths as an industrial location more important priorities than climate targets.

Innovation, then, has happened and petrol and diesel engines have become notably more economical. But because of weak reduction targets and heavier and higher-performance cars, this innovative potential has not come anywhere close to being fully utilised; in fact, it has been inhibited. Innovations do not evolve in a vacuum but are shaped by power structures, short-term economic interests and cultural orientations. And a further problem comes into play: innovations until now have been geared towards individual private vehicles. So the existing transport model is being made more efficient but it is not being systematically questioned or even overhauled. There is no "transport transition" in sight. The same applies to the two big new stories that are now being spun by politics and industry: the electric car and the driverless vehicle. Both facilitate the perpetuation of the current model with new means — and in the process, directly constrain the horizon of innovation.

In such a context, it is unrealistic to assume that technological evolution can remain neutral and not be shaped by interests and power.

"If I had asked people what they wanted, they would have said faster horses," was Henry Ford's succinct description of mental path dependency. This same phenomenon applies to today's automobile or aviation industries. What we can expect from them are faster or more fuel efficient vehicles, but not a different transportation model.

The market and technology fixation of Green Economy tends to exclude other avenues of exploration. If the aim is to push back "the car's sweeping seizure of power",[126] then different enabling conditions and policies are needed. No technological advance and no market mechanism will lead there automatically. Or, in other words, if we rely on the path paved by technology and the market, then certain decisions have already been made, namely, not to depart from the path, to keep pursuing it, and to "decarbonise" it at the most.

The task of building "increasingly efficient cars" is a very different matter from the systematic promotion of public transport, the suppression of the car in central areas of our cities, or a strategy that prioritises avoiding and reducing private car-use. Any such option definitely needs a different approach than the position upheld by probably the most powerful German industry, whose mindset seems hot-wired into the mental structures and desires of large parts of the population.

The limits to efficiency
and the illusion of decoupling

Many of the trends described here are also discussed in terms of a "rebound effect": efficiency gains lead to savings which often result in different, resource-intensive expenditures, and these, in turn, negate the savings and efficiency effects. For example, someone could use the amount saved by driving a low-consumption vehicle to take a flight to Paris. This is called an indirect rebound effect. A direct rebound effect is when the higher energy efficiency itself induces the purchase of certain goods. Finally an automatic dryer is purchased because the new generation of appliances does not consume as much energy, or garden lighting is installed with energy-saving bulbs. The rebound effect relativises the success of efficiency strategies; this is now generally acknowledged. To what extent this occurs, however, is a matter on which there are very divergent views, and the calculations are not beyond dispute. One EU-commissioned study finds that the direct rebound effect "eats up" around 10 to 30 per cent of efficiency gains.[127] The ecology expert Tilman Santarius comes to a different conclusion: "From several meta studies […] which summarise and evaluate hundreds of individual studies on the rebound effect, it can be deduced that rebound effects will, in the long run, consume at least 50 per cent of the savings potential of efficiency measures."[128]

One may argue about the exact figures; what matters is that the rebound effect throws a bucket of cold water on all those who believe that absolute decoupling can be achieved through greater efficiency and green growth alone. What would be the consequence, for example, if the one-litre car,[129] introduced by Renault, became an affordable reality? A possible outcome might be a massive increase in sales figures and even more cars on the road. Is that what we want?[130]

The rebound-effect debate brings up to date the central question in the context of innovation and growth: can we continue to improve our prosperity without raising the consumption of resources and the emission of CO_2 and other greenhouse gases? Or to reframe the question, is the decoupling of growth and consumption possible? In answering this question, it is important to differentiate between relative and absolute decoupling. In the latter case, consumption would not only have to rise more slowly than growth, but actually to fall in absolute figures. The dilemma can be illustrated very well with the example of private households: Electrical devices have become more and more efficient over the last few years, but energy consumption has risen, nevertheless, because increasing numbers of devices were purchased. A relative decoupling is undoubtedly possible, and is already happening. Evidence can be seen, for instance in the statistics about the CO_2-intensity of gross domestic product (GDP).[131] Based on the example of CO_2-intensity, the economist Tim Jackson has developed an "arithmetic of growth".[132] Jackson shows that the carbon-intensity of 768 (world average) would have to fall to 36 in the year 2050 if the aim were to limit global warming to a 2 °C rise. This means that intensity would have to fall by seven per cent per year, i.e. ten times faster than is currently the case in Germany. And this scenario still omits to consider that large parts of the world must achieve income gains in order to overcome poverty. Jackson reckons that carbon intensity would have to drop to 14, if one grants an income at the EU-level of 2007 to the whole world in the year 2050. Jackson presented his figures in 2009. In 2014, the consulting firm PricewaterhouseCoopers (PwC) — not suspected of any radical critique of growth — came to similar conclusions.[133] According to PwC, the global economy must attain a reduction in carbon intensity of 6.2 per cent per annum in order to meet the climate target. The most recent figures (2013) show a rate of only 1.2 per cent. And every year that we do not accomplish 6.2 per cent, the figure for the subsequent years rises. So, although progress has been made, over the last six years the gap between what we are achieving and what we ought to do has grown larger — as PwC clearly underlines. And all this after years of intensive policy to reduce the emission of CO_2 and successful efforts to increase efficiency.

Very similar conclusions are drawn by the environmental scientist Vaclav Smil, whose book, *Making the Modern World*, published in 2014, is a monumental and very current overview of the materials of the modern world: "Innovation *is* making products more energy-efficient — but then we consume so many more products that there's been no absolute dematerialization of anything. We still consume more steel, more aluminum, more glass, and so on. As long as we're on this endless material cycle, this merry-go-round, well, technical innovation cannot keep pace."[134]

As the arithmetic of growth shows, the assumption that growth is possible in parallel with an absolute reduction of CO_2 emissions and resource consumption requires a level of optimism that borders on magical thinking. Naturally, relative decoupling is possible, but it is insufficient to achieve climate targets. "The truth is that there is as yet no credible, socially just, ecologically sustainable scenario of continually growing incomes for a world of nine billion people."[135] This statement is confirmed by the new statistics.

Therefore, the starting point of Green Economy, which is to postulate growth and innovation and to brush away any problematisation of growth, is troubling. Should we not instead be asking: how can we achieve environmental sustainability and (greater) social justice? What growth is desirable? And what growth should preferably be halted? Questions like these have been discussed for 30 years in environmental economics, taken up by Green politics, and thought through for individual sectors (the energy, agricultural and transport transformation). Equally, in the political and discursive debate about international climate and resource equity, there are a host of approaches dating back to the 1992 Earth Summit in Rio de Janeiro, if not earlier, which emphasise that the global North must change course and shrink to make development and growth in the global South possible at all, in view of climate change and increasingly scarce resources. This is a discussion that we will not elaborate on here, however.[136]

Land use – a new green revolution

Agriculture occupies a key position in all designs for a sustainable future or a Green Economy. The necessity of switching the fossil-based energy model to renewable sources presents new and colossal challenges for agricultural production, forestry, and land use in its entirety.

The prime concern is the food security of the nine billion people who, according to UN estimates, will be living on Earth by the year 2050. Unfortunately, this fact is often brought into play as a terrifying scenario or as justification for advancing the agroindustrial intensification of farming and the expansion of land use. When it comes to land-use strategies, food security for the poor and hungry of this world is not generally in the foreground,[137] but the question of how to serve the growing consumption demands of the new global middle class. The middle class has the purchasing power, and so there is more money to be made from them. In many regions of the world, we are witnessing the replacement of fossil fuels with biomass. As a consequence, productive land is being expanded for farmed fuels and electricity generation. Agriculture, along with forestry, also supplies important feedstocks (biomass) for the chemical industry, among others. The 1.5 °C limit enshrined in the Paris Agreement represents for many an additional pressure on land, if biomass-based carbon sequestration (BECCS) were to become applied to create "negative emissions" (see below for that debate).

In Germany, biomass accounts for a sizeable share of the energy mix. This is often underestimated. In 2013, almost as much electricity was generated from biomass, namely 47.3 terawatt hours (TWh), as from wind energy, which generated 51.7 TWh. Biomass also provides the lion's share of renewable energies for heat generation. Solid biomass and biogas account for 104.5 TWh in that segment, while solar thermal output only amounts to 6.8 TWh. And beyond that, biomass makes a contribution to fuel production, although this trend is declining slightly. In the year 2013, farmed fuels (the German Federal Environmental Agency refers to them as biofuels) accounted for a 5.5 per cent share, which equates to a substantial 34.3 TWh.[138]

If we look not just at electricity generation but at the contribution of renewable energies to total energy generation, then wood as an energy source—slightly archaic as it may sound—contributes more than wind energy. In the EU-27 wood is responsible for 38.9 per cent[139] of sustainable energies; worldwide the figure is 70 per cent, whereas other biomass only amounts to seven per cent.[140]

This considerable existing proportion of farmed industrial feedstocks would expand further in all Green Economy scenarios. And not only that: wind and solar energy, the expansion of which is a key strategic aim, also require additional land. The departure from fossil energy enhances the value of land-based energy sources. This is the clearly observable trend so far, and it is set to continue. So the question of how land is used acquires new dimensions and conflict lines. How to safeguard the nourishment of humankind in view of these developments is a pivotal task for the future.

The answers in the Green Economy mainstream are as predictable as the challenge is obvious: a new "Green Revolution" must come to pass. The reference to the historical green revolution is intentional. It is cited time and time again as an example to illustrate the possibility of drastic increases in agricultural yields. Thus, the New Climate Economy Report reads: "Much of the progress we have made since the period of catastrophic famines in Asia and Africa in the 1970s and earlier is due to extraordinary increases in agricultural productivity, driven by the 'Green Revolution', a concerted, multi-decade effort to modernise farming in the developing world. High-yield varieties of rice, wheat and maize were developed and widely distributed, and the use of agricultural inputs (irrigation, fertilisers) sharply increased. Across Asia, average rice yields nearly doubled, and wheat yields nearly tripled."[141]

The fact that this statement is not referenced with scientific sources but claimed as a fact—an article in *The Economist* magazine serves as evidence—shows that this is not about scientific debate but a contest of narratives.

Yield increases per hectare owing to new varieties and higher inputs — that is, in a nutshell, the purported success story of the Green Revolution. It glosses over many questions, however. The historical Green Revolution was also based on significantly higher use of synthetic fertiliser combined with huge fossil energy inputs, resulting in a drastic rise in nitrogen loading. The Green Revolution can also be seen as an enrichment of soil fertility with fossil resources — which, in itself, underscores that a strategy aimed specifically at replacing fossil resources cannot possibly pick up the legacy of the Green Revolution.

Critical to the success of the Green Revolution was the increased use of synthetic fertiliser, so it also exemplifies that there are not always win-win solutions, but rather, that new dilemmas and negative social and ecological effects can arise with any technological innovation. The huge worldwide rise in yields per hectare (not just within the scope of the Green Revolution) correlates with an enormous growth in nitrogen use (as a fertiliser) in agriculture, which has led to one of the most severe types of environmental pollution in the world and tied modern agriculture to the use of fossil energy.

Now, a new "Green Revolution" is intent on repeating the raising of per-hectare yields, again with intensified inputs such as the blanket use of herbicides in combination with genetically modified crops. The genetics industry never tires of proclaiming its front-line role in combating hunger.

However, this fixation on boosting per-hectare yields masks other crucial questions completely: who is producing what for whom, and how? Which needs are we taking as given, and how much lifestyle is negotiable? "Agriculture currently produces roughly one-third more calories in arithmetical terms than would be needed to feed everyone, and food production is still growing faster than the world population."[142] Hunger, then, is not primarily a problem of production but of access to food and land. Not only is land unequally distributed, land requirements for nutrition also differ enormously.

Europe's food supply is dependent upon using land outside its borders — and on a gigantic scale. This is primarily due to the import

Haber-Bosch and the Green Revolution

Rarely has an invention been as influential as the ammonia synthesis process developed by Fritz Haber and Carl Bosch. The Haber-Bosch process enabled nitrogen to be produced on an industrial scale, allowing the extensive use of chemical fertiliser, which became the key pillar of modern agriculture and led to its massive increase in productivity in the 20th century.

However, it is the Green Revolution of the 1960s and 1970s which is, perhaps, lodged more firmly in the public's collective memory, for this was not only an agricultural but also a public relations success story. The "father" of this Green Revolution was the agronomist Norman Borlaug, who won a Nobel Prize in 1970 — but not for chemistry, like Haber and Bosch. Instead, Borlaug won the Nobel Peace Prize, for he is widely reported to have saved millions of people from starvation. There are undoubtedly many points of contact between the historic Green Revolution and Green Economy. The Green Revolution centred on the development of high-yield varieties; IR8 was particularly well-known and was hailed as "miracle rice". The figures attesting to its success are impressive: In India, rice production doubled between 1965 and 1980, and in Indonesia, rice yield increased from 1.3 tonnes per hectare (t/ha) in 1960 to 4.3 t/ha in 1994.[143] However, the use of chemical fertilisers soared at the same time: in Indonesia, for example, it rose from 25 kg in 1975 to 150 kg per hectare today. The high-yield varieties generally only work in combination with artificial fertilisers and irrigation, which is why Indian ecologist and women's rights activist Vandana Shiva has suggested that it may be appropriate to use the term "highly-responsive varieties" (HRVs), given that the high yields can only be achieved through the interaction with fertilisers. Certainly, the success of industrial agriculture is not simply the story of a miracle achieved with new cultivars, but is more contentious, for this success was achieved through a complex process involving seeds, mechanisation, fertilisers and irrigation. Even today, assessments of the Green Revolution vary widely and provoke impassioned responses: "This agricultural revolution quadrupled yields and pushed down the price of food, but it led to agriculture's dependency on fossil fuels and turned it into a major polluter."[144]

But rice — the flagship of the Green Revolution — shows that viable alternatives do exist. The System of Rice Intensification (SRI) is probably the most important example of an ecologically inspired approach to the modernisation of agriculture that requires less input but achieves greater output. It is a different way of thinking about innovation; it does not work miracles. "Switching to SRI requires a lot of courage, especially in areas where the survival of families depends on the rice harvest. The method requires a lot of work and knowledge, for example it is difficult for many small-scale farmers to irrigate the fields at the perfect moment. Nevertheless, 4 to 5 million farmers in over 50 countries in Asia, Africa and Latin America are now applying SRI. In China and India, authorities are already promoting the method. 'I think that SRI is something unprecedented, as very few previous innovations have shown such a huge productivity windfall. And just as surprising is the fact that we have been able to proceed on such an international scale with so little support and so much opposition,' says Uphoff.[145] Opposition came primarily from the International Rice Research Institute (IRRI) in the Philippines, a research centre administered by the World Bank. According to some scientists the method is too labour-intensive and the increase in yields is not sufficiently verified. Seed and agrochemical companies are also not supporters of a method which lures away clients by reducing the need for seeds, fertiliser and pesticides. But SRI is spreading rapidly: More than 300 scientific articles have been published on SRI."[146] ■

of meat and feedstuffs. This enormous land consumption for meat production is the elephant in the room — it is impossible to overlook and is much discussed, yet politics refuses to acknowledge the consequences. No single action would make a greater contribution to relieving the pressure on agricultural land than the reduction of meat consumption. Plus, further growth in this area is not really conceivable. The fixation on raising yields per hectare blinds us to the fact that, apart from all the ecological consequences, a new Green Revolution with its novel technologies presupposes a socially formed model of land use, which is based on extreme inequalities and which will exacerbate these even further.

No sign of a miracle

The hope that all our problems can be solved by some new supertechnology is nothing new; and even past disappointments have not been able to eliminate such expectations. Even far less radical visions of the future still often turn on hopes of technological salvation.

In the modern era, the mother of all hopes of technological salvation is surely the use of nuclear fission for energy generation. In 1956, Gerhard Löwenthal — later known for hosting the conservative *ZDF Magazin* on West German television — published a book that was symptomatically entitled: *Wir werden durch Atome leben* (We will live by virtue of atoms). The enthusiasm for nuclear technology cut across all political camps. Ernst Bloch, a Marxist philosopher who had fled from the German Democratic Republic, waxed lyrical: "Nuclear energy creates fertile land from desert, springtime from ice. A few hundred pounds of uranium and thorium would suffice to make the Sahara and the Gobi Desert disappear, to transform Siberia and North America, Greenland and the Antarctic into Riviera." Meanwhile the German Social Democratic Party (SPD) dreamed of far more than cheap energy: "Nuclear energy can become a blessing for hundreds of millions of people whose lives are still blighted" it stated in the SPD nuclear plan of 1956. By "raising prosperity for all, nuclear energy can decisively help to consolidate democracy internally and peace among the nations."[147]

The post-war period was hailed as the nuclear age. The concept even found its way into the preamble of the SPD's Godesberg Programme of 1959.[148] The Federal Republic of Germany established a Nuclear Ministry; its first minister was Franz Josef Strauss. In 1958, Ford unveiled the Nucleon, the prototype of a nuclear-powered car. In Europe, Simca did the same with the futuristic Fulgur. A little earlier, in 1955, the world saw the Soviet Union close to producing a nuclear-powered truck based on the "Iron Bison".[149]

Today, such plans appear ridiculous; but it is good to be reminded of them. Nevertheless, it would be wrong to reduce the history of nuclear energy merely to the dashing of great expectations. The generation of energy through nuclear fission has been technologically realised, and nuclear power has come to command an important, although not dominant, place in supplying the world's energy. According to the figures in the Energy Outlook, the share of worldwide electricity generation contributed by nuclear energy is about eleven per cent; it did, at one time, reach 18 per cent.[150]

France accomplished one of the most impressive energy transformations in the history of humankind within a few years: between 1979 and 1990, when nuclear power's share of energy generation rose from 20 per cent to 75 per cent. But despite impressive successes, technological maturation and global diffusion, nuclear energy did not achieve the great breakthrough. There are several reasons for this: the vulnerability of the technology to accidents was drastically underestimated, as were the costs. Nuclear power plants are extremely expensive to build and produce hazardous wastes for which there is no means of disposal. For the insurance industry, this is a nightmare. Soon it became impossible to advocate nuclear energy as the magic bullet of the modern era; at best it was a problematic tool. Obviously, the problems were significantly underestimated or kept quiet during the first phase of development. The history of nuclear power is by no means over, but even the quite pro-nuclear International Energy Agency (IEA) sees only limited potential for its future.

Nuclear energy's promise of salvation is not quite consigned to the past; it lives on in the hopes attached to nuclear fusion. Once again, the proponents dream of a clean, inexhaustible source of energy. One single gram of the hydrogen isotopes used, deuterium and tritium, is capable of supplying as much energy as eleven tonnes of coal. The ITER research facility in France is considered the world's most expensive research project. Over time the originally budgeted 4.5 billion euros have escalated to 15 billion. But it remains uncertain whether nuclear fusion can ever produce energy on a large scale at costs the market can bear.

A completely unintended aspect in the history of nuclear power, however, is the fact that it generated what is probably the most important environmental movement. Almost everywhere that nuclear power stations were built, resistance developed. Nobody anticipated this but it is an important lesson for any approach that is fixated on technological innovations: there is the subjective factor, not just a power constellation—technologies often meet with resistance, and this resistance is not just a futile rebellion against inevitable progress, but often wins the day and influences at least how innovations are implemented.

This is by no means applicable to all technologies: the mobile phone gained acceptance despite a certain amount of scepticism and some turned-up noses from the cultural pessimists, and hardly anyone today prefers a black-and-white television set. But risk-laden technologies, in particular, have become the object of societal debates. This is not confined to nuclear energy; genetic engineering is also extremely controversial. Both technologies are associated with a production model: the nuclear industry can only be realised with large-scale projects, massive state support and large energy corporations; and genetic engineering not only produces food but also requires the large-scale production of monocultures, and the marketing of certain technologies from which the large agribusiness firms derive benefits. Technologies are not just neutral instruments; they are the expression of power relations, they determine and influence development paths, and for that very reason they are contested, and rightly so.

What is nanotechnology?

Size does matter — this could be nanotechnology's tagline. It is conducted at the nanoscale between one atom and *100 nanometres*. A nanometre is *one*-billionth of a metre (10^{-9}). At the nanoscale, the physical properties of materials change, so nanotechnology offers untold opportunities to develop nanoparticles for specific purposes or to alter the properties of existing materials. Indeed, nanoparticles are already being manufactured for commercial applications, especially in the cosmetics industry. According to the German Federal Ministry of Education and Research, nanotechnology is one of the most important key technologies of our time. However, it also raises questions: what risks are posed by new materials, which have undergone manipulation at the nanoscale? ▪

Another technology that was launched amid great hopes and promises is nanotechnology. This is partly due to the possibilities of the technology itself, but also to the eloquent pronouncements of Eric Drexler, who is generally known as the "father" (some say "godfather") of nanotechnology: "What if nanotechnology could deliver on its original promise — not only new, useful, nanoscale products, but a new, transformative production technology able to displace industrial production technologies and bring radical improvements in production cost, scope, and resource efficiency? What if we could raise the global material standard of living above that of today's richest nations, while reducing impacts on Earth's environment? What if we could manage a more rapid transition to zero net carbon emissions, and (yet more challenging) could afford to build the systems that would be required to capture, compress, and remove a trillion or so tonnes of industrial-era CO_2 from the atmosphere?"[151]

This was Drexler's description of how he saw the potentials of nanotechnology in 2013. Unlike nuclear fusion, nanotechnology has been developed through to practical use. Items produced by means of nanotechnology are found in everyday products, particularly cosmetics. But massive financial support and extensive research have not turned nanotechnology into a magic bullet for everything. Promises and hopes are naturally also part of a strategy to mobilise money, which nanotechnology has accomplished par excellence. But in the meantime, the prospect of nanotechnology becoming the great "game changer" has given way to more realistic perspectives. And attention to the risks of nanotechnology has increased.[152] In particular, nanotechnology has not been able to honour one promise that initially also attracted many ecologists, namely, that it could contribute to dematerialisation on a relevant scale of magnitude.

In the absence of the great breakthrough of a miracle technology, in recent years we have still experienced a phenomenal improvement of existing technologies. Solar energy and wind power have become considerably more efficient, radically reducing their generation costs. Likewise, coal-fired power plants have become "cleaner" and more efficient. At the same time, new technologies are facilitating the exploitation of new gas and oil deposits. Thus technological progress is not paving the way for renewable energy only, by any means. Technological progress — such as CO_2 compression — augurs a significant future for coal and petroleum as well.

All that remains to be remarked is that we cannot foresee the future, that many promises of new technologies have not been fulfilled, and that many a prince has turned into a frog. Time after time, the risks and negative consequences of new technologies have been systematically underestimated during their initial phase. Next, we will therefore discuss a new field of innovation, synthetic biology, which has so far barely been a topic of public debate — although it receives billions in public research funding.

Synthetic biology –
new promises and old power structures

Synthetic biology[153] — or "extreme genetic engineering", as others say — promises more than innovation: *How Synthetic Biology Will Reinvent Nature and Ourselves* is the title of the agenda-setting book by George Church, who ranks alongside Craig Venter as the most popular and publicly effective prophet of synthetic biology. In truth, it is no small agenda. Synthetic biology goes much further than "classic" genetic engineering. It not only aims to genetically modify lifeforms but to reassemble them or even design completely new ones. The idea that one can, in principle, build a kind of mini-factory out of every bacteria, every microbe and every alga, which when fed with almost any form of biomass can produce everything possible (for example fuel, plastic, vanilla aroma, etc.), goes far beyond the classic methods of genetic engineering. Such a vision comprises an entirely new mode of production and hence also a different economy — one which ultimately casts nature as an inexhaustible factory and humans as the masters of nature and all its processes. The concept "natural" will become meaningless. Such a world will keep turning with very few workers. Microbes and algae will do the job instead.

The "holy grail" of synthetic biology has always been the manufacturing of next-generation biofuels on a large scale. In recent years, therefore, the large carbon technology groups and countless international energy and chemical corporations, including Shell, Exxon, BP, Chevron, Total, Petrobras, BASF, Dow and DuPont, have invested billions in small and larger start-up corporations from Silicon Valley. Due to numerous technical problems (especially in ramping up production), the industry has increasingly turned to different products in recent years, focusing on "high value" and "low volume" such as aromatics and additives for the cosmetics industry. Whereas, until a few years ago, mainly mass-produced chemicals, bioplastics and bio-fuels were on the market, in the last few years they have been joined by such products as synthetic vanilla flavour manufactured by Evolva, artemisinin (an anti-malaria substance) from Amyris or lauric acid (for use in soaps) from Solazyme. Examples of other synthesised compounds close to launch or already launched are rose oil, stevia, sandalwood, saffron and milk protein.

Understandably, the defence and health ministries are also taking a great interest in synthetic biology: to invent new medical and military wonder weapons, or to defend against those of the enemy.

It is a highly dynamic branch of industry, yet resistance is also growing. An example: the Belgian detergent and cleaning-agent manufacturer Ecover announced that it would be replacing some of the palm kernel oil in its products with algae oil. Palm kernel oil is derived from the kernels of the oil palm, and palm oil from the fruits of the tree. One of the arguments used by detergent manufacturers like Ecover to justify this is the ecological gain, if harmful palm oil production can be reduced. It can be assumed, however, that the production of the necessary biomass (sugar) to feed the algae will to a very great extent compensate for the anticipated reduction in land area.[154] However, even if there is a net saving in land area — the oil is produced by algae whose genes have been modified using the techniques of synthetic biology. So, there is a risk, with ostensibly good intentions, of legitimising a risky and relatively untested technology which then can also be used for quite different purposes. After massive protests from NGOs, however, Ecover has put these plans on ice for the time being.

The risks and problems associated with synbio research and application are vast and diverse. Its medical application certainly requires separate studies, and we therefore will not examine it here — even though it is currently a major field of research. With reference to the research and application of synthetic biology for the manufacture of fuels, plastic, aromatics and other products in the context of bioeconomics, the following issue areas are crucial:

♦ Synthetic biology produces self-reproducing organisms, which are either released into the environment or else brought into use in supposedly closed laboratories or factories. In both cases, the safety risk is enormous. The possible consequences for humans and the environment of contamination with synthetically manufactured organisms or genetic material are currently unforeseeable.

◆ Products produced by means of synthetic biology (for example, additives in foods or cosmetics) need not be labelled, as things currently stand; they are deemed to be "natural". The result is a massive deception of consumers, plus millions of people in the South will lose their livelihoods, if synthetic vanilla or synthetic coconut oil substitutes force the equivalent agricultural products off the market. In the Philippines, for example, 25 million people are directly or indirectly dependent on the coconut industry.[155]

◆ Even synthetic biology cannot produce something out of nothing. The bacteria, algae and microbes need something to feed on. So far, sugar has primarily served this purpose. Therefore, many companies in the synbio sector also own large sugarcane plantations or refineries in countries including Brazil. However, sugar — like other agricultural products — is traded on the global market and its price is subject to the dictates of supply and demand. High demand for sugar leads to a price increase and ultimately results in sugarcane being planted on many land areas that were previously used for food production or the clearance of forested land. It therefore remains to be seen whether the net gain in land area from the use of, for example, palm kernel oil substitutes is really so positive. Even if research manages to substitute sugar with wood or perhaps, in future, with any form of biomass, the fact remains that biomass production requires land, water and other natural resources and thus enters into direct competition with the production of foods for a constantly growing global population.

Certainly that much is clear to those firms who are now investing heavily in the kind of research that will place synthetic biology at the service of the fossil industry. This trend is especially remarkable since many synbio corporations have explicitly presented them-

Synthetic vanilla – a natural product?

Natural vanillin is obtained from the vanilla orchid. Synthetic biology vanillin is distinct from the artificial vanillin already on the market, although both are engineered in labs. Artificial vanillin is a mix of chemical components. The new synbio vanillin is synthesised by a genetically modified organism — a GMO yeast engineered using synthetic biology techniques. To create this synbio yeast, synthetic DNA is designed on a computer and inserted into the DNA of naturally occurring yeast. This is very different from traditional methods of selectively breeding naturally occurring yeast for various purposes, such as brewing beer or baking bread. In selective breeding, no foreign genetic matter that does not occur naturally in yeast is inserted into the yeast genome. The synbio yeast is fed sugar and biosynthesises vanillin through a fermentation process. Even though this vanillin is engineered and created by a pathway that does not exist in nature, the synbio company Evolva and its partner, International Flavors and Fragrances, are marketing synbio vanillin as "natural."[156] An estimated 200,000 people are involved in the production of cured vanilla beans per annum. Madagascar, Comoros and Réunion historically account for around three quarters of the world's vanilla bean production. The global vanilla market, both natural and chemically-derived (vanillin), is valued at about $650 million. The value of worldwide trade in vanilla beans amounted to $150 million in 2013. At the consumer end, natural vanilla sells for thousands of dollars per kilogramme, while synthetic vanillin sells for only tens of dollars. Production of natural vanilla from vanilla beans is extremely labour intensive: 1 kg of vanilla requires approximately 500 kg of vanilla pods and hand pollination of approximately 40,000 flowers. Vanilla bean production and processing is a vital cash crop in agroforestry systems where there are few alternative income sources. In Madagascar, an estimated 80,000 families cultivate vanilla orchids on approximately 30,000 hectares. In Comoros, about 5,000–10,000 families depend on vanilla bean production. Approximately 10,000 farming families cultivate vanilla orchids in Mexico, the geographic centre of origin of vanilla.[157]

selves as alternatives to the fossil future. In part this involves the use of methane, derived from the extraction of natural gas and oil by means of fracking, as a substitute for sugar or other biomass. Such use would hugely boost the gas's value, which would certainly be of benefit to the corporate groups in view of the low oil price. Secondly, it involves the use of synthetically manufactured microorganisms in the exploitation of hard to access oil and gas reserves. For while the easily accessible reserves of oil are dwindling, what remains is more and more residual oil that the corporations are attempting to exploit by means of various techniques, which collectively go by the name of "enhanced oil recovery". One such technique, which is increasingly taking off, is "microbial enhanced hydrocarbon recovery" (MEHR). Microorganisms are "programmed" accordingly and injected into the rocks, where certain chemicals they produce flush out the oil or prepare it for extraction (and later also transportation). More than 300 trials are known to have taken place. Corporations like BP, Shell and Statoil are investing in this technique.[158]

Another new playground for synthetic biology is the field of so-called "climate-smart agriculture". The UN's Food and Agriculture Organization (FAO) began talking about climate-smart agriculture in 2009 as a way to bring agriculture — and its role in mitigation, adaptation and food security — into the climate negotiations. The Global Alliance for Climate-Smart Agriculture (GACSA) was formally launched in 2014, its membership now including 22 national governments, agribusiness lobby groups (the majority representing the fertiliser industry), the world's largest network of public agricultural scientists — the Consultative Group on International Agricultural Research (CGIAR) — universities and NGOs. Climate-smart agriculture is also promoted by the World Business Council for Sustainable Development (WBCSD) through its Low Carbon Technology Partnerships Initiative (LCTPi).

Potential and existing applications of synthetic biology in this context include public and private research projects to alter the process of photosynthesis in plants and microbes (theoretically to increase the carbon sequestration of plants), projects that aim to increase nitrogen absorption in plants and create "self-fertilising plants" (theoretically to reduce fertiliser applications), new SynBio applications developed by agrochemical giant Syngenta that make the activation of "climate-tolerance" traits dependent on the application of proprietary pesticides (thereby tying farmers closer to agrochemical use), and proposals to release controversial "Gene Drive" technology into the wild to make weed populations more susceptible to Monsanto's Roundup herbicide, altering ecosystems to extend the commercial viability of that agrochemical.[159]

One very fundamental problematic issue is that the synbio companies are securing patents which come into the category of "patents on life". So far synthetic biology has been a largely unregulated field. The main corporations profiting are almost exclusively based in the USA, Japan, Canada, New Zealand, Brazil and in Europe. Those countries' governments represent the interests of these corporations in international forums, such as during the negotiation of bilateral free trade and investment treaties, for example.

Interestingly, at the Conference of the Parties to the United Nations Convention on Biological Diversity held in October 2014 in South Korea, a small but decisive breakthrough was achieved: the governments undertook to create regulations and to examine the risks to food security, biodiversity and health, among other aspects. To prevent this process initiated by civil society from degenerating into farce, the critics of synthetic biology certainly have their work cut out over the next few years. At the same time they are faced with powerful opponents who will give their all to defend their power.

Whilst many protagonists of synthetic biology are advertising on talk shows, in colourful brochures and on their websites how they first design the DNA as "bio bricks" on the computer, where they can then dismantle and reassemble it like a type of Lego, the real science of biology is developing in a different direction. The last few years have taught genetics that the main thing we know is that we do not know everything, by far. DNA is very much more complex than was assumed until quite recently. Pieces of information take effect across various genes and interlace with one another. What actually happens when we chop DNA into pieces and put it back together differently like a giant construction kit, nobody can predict with any accuracy.

So why, then, are so many corporations and governments — especially from the USA, Great Britain, France, the Netherlands, Denmark, Switzerland, Germany, Canada, China, Brazil, Japan and Australia — investing so much money? Even large private foundations such as the Bill & Melinda Gates Foundation, the Sloan Foundation and the Gordon and Betty Moore Foundation are investing large sums. Might this be a case of a financial bubble? One can only speculate about that. Many aspects of the great vision of bioeconomics based on synthetic biology controlled by humans will certainly not be realisable. Going by the products that are already on the market, significant disadvantages for food security, livelihoods, biodiversity and climate change can already be discerned. This shows that we cannot afford not to care about what is being researched and tested in the context and in the name of a Bioeconomy.

Geoengineering the climate

Would it not be wonderful if we could halt and even reverse climate change without having to change anything — so that we could cheerfully carry on flying, driving and burning coal without a guilty conscience?

The idea of geoengineering suggests that such a solution is feasible. It blends grandiose and crackpot ideas like gigantic mirrors in space or artificial volcanoes (to reduce solar radiation) with very much more localised yet large-scale manipulations of the global climate system: fertilisation of the oceans or broad-scale planting of trees or other forms of biomass (to remove additional CO_2 from the atmosphere).

Even the Intergovernmental Panel on Climate Change (IPCC) included geoengineering in the list of possible climate change mitigation measures in its fifth and most recent assessment report in 2014, effectively making the concept respectable.[160] The desire for quick and easy solutions derives on the one hand from desperation in the face of rapidly accelerating climate change and the incapacity of almost all governments to tackle it politically. On the other hand, however, those investing in geoengineering research are precisely those corporations and governments who would have everything to lose by departing from the fossil development model. Large petroleum firms like Shell, Exxon or Chevron have sunk considerable sums into research and lobbying for "carbon capture and storage" (CCS), i.e. the injection of carbon dioxide into geological voids. What is ultimately at stake is a free pass to continue burning fossil fuels — a Plan B for climate change mitigation which could devastate any efforts to accomplish Plan A. Since the Paris Agreement has made it utterly clear that Plan A with business as usual will fall far short of bringing us anywhere close to a "safe climate", for many the mentioning of the famous 1.5 °C limit in the Paris Agreement opens the door to a much more favourable reception of geoengineering.

The position at the outset is the assumption that we will fall short of our climate targets and can only arrive at "net zero emissions" by generating "negative emissions". This will require new technologies, which for the most part have not yet even been developed. In view of the central importance of land-use changes and the role of biomass in the debate surrounding Green Economy, we home in on a particular geoengineering process which is increasingly viewed as a sustainable option in the context of international climate policy: BECCS.[161]

"Bioenergy with carbon capture and storage" (BECCS) is the flagship for the new approach of net zero emissions, which is supposed to justify exceeding the Earth's biocapacity. This clearly signals that in the context of geoengineering, as elsewhere, the question of land use is crucial! BECCS schemes involve planting trees or other biomass on a broad scale so as to absorb CO_2; later these are burnt for the purpose of generating electricity, and the CO_2 then released is stored. All that is certain is that such a strategy would intensify the policy of land-take.

However, simple arithmetic shows that these are not serious proposals, but chimeras: to draw one billion tonnes of CO_2 from the atmosphere by means of BECCS, scientists estimate that 218 to 990 million hectares would have to be planted (estimate based on switchgrass).[162] That is 14 to 65 times as much land as the USA currently uses to produce maize for the extraction of ethanol. In addition, nitrous oxide emissions arising from the fertiliser inputs that would be necessary for the cropping of this land could further exacerbate climate change. What is more, vast CO_2 emissions must be taken into account, which would arise from the clearance of trees, bushes and grass from several hundred million hectares of land, the destruction of large carbon sinks in the soil, and the transportation and processing of the biomass.

Even more problematic is the idea that the compressed CO_2 could be pumped into old oil wells for storage, which creates an additional financial incentive for more petroleum drilling, irrespective of how high the costs are. The US Energy Ministry estimates that, using such methods, 67 billion barrels of oil — triple the volume of known US oil reserves — could be drilled economically. Considering how much money is involved, this could be one of the motives behind pro-BECCS lobbying work in reality. What is certain is that no form of CO_2 capture and storage advances the objective of structural change towards complete decarbonisation.

What is most disconcerting is the fact that none of the IPCC scenarios that bring us close enough to limiting warming to 2 °C (let alone 1.5 °C) work without an implicit use of BECCS or other negative emission technologies.[163] Remembering that Working Group 3 of the IPCC is run by economists tasked by our governments to preserve our economic system in a climate-safe future, there are only two possible conclusions: we must either surrender our ecological objectives and thereby the lives of millions of people on Earth or dare to begin to question the very fundamental structures and beliefs our economic system is built upon.

Technological innovations – a tentative synthesis

Our brief journey through the world of technological innovations reveals a landscape that is fissured and multifaceted. While some are working on more economical diesel engines, others are trying to rewrite the history of evolution. The concept of "innovation" is clearly open to very divergent interpretations. Synthesis and subsequent evaluation are fraught with difficulty. It is beyond dispute, however, that innovations proceed and are vital to a sustainable future. We certainly do not seek to cast general suspicion upon "innovation" from a perspective of cultural criticism. Yet, equally, innovation cannot be stylised as a panacea. Therefore, it is important not to talk only about generic innovation as a cipher of the future, but rather about specific innovations in their unique contexts.

One of the most significant historians and theoreticians of innovation, David Edgerton, developed a comprehensive critique of "innovation-centred narratives" of technologies. In his major work, *The Shock of the Old*, he attempts a nuanced analysis of the teleological view that "innovation leads to a better world". One aspect is especially important: "Our obsession with innovation also blinds us to how much of technology is focussed on keeping things the same."[164]

New technologies like CCS are intended to prolong the fossil age, not to supersede it. Much the same is true of innovations in the automobile industry. Particularly in light of the Volkswagen emissions scandal, many will be surprised to learn that the corporation that invests most in research and development worldwide is Volkswagen and has topped the "Global Innovation 1000" list for years. Among the top twenty, there are no fewer than six car firms.[165]

To assess how innovations may support Green Economy, a number of comments can be made on the basis of past experience:

1. Technological innovations have not worked any miracles so far — particularly not with regard to energy and material consumption. The nuclear industry has not solved our energy problem; nor has nanotechnology contributed substantially to dematerialisation of the economy. Miracles or disruptive innovations, i.e. innovations which completely revolutionise a branch of the economy, are possible of course, but no strategy for the future can rationally be built upon them. It would be like trying to plan one's life on the basis of a future lottery win — which is, after all, definitely possible. Disruptive innovations are rather to be observed in sub-areas: in the consumer mass market, digital cameras are replacing analogue ones, and tube televisions are on the way out. The energy problem is much more complex than that.

2. Many technological innovations have pursued paths that amplify problems or create new ones. Agrofuels are the best example. The issues go far beyond the question whether to produce food or fuel. Reducing the emissions of private cars by producing agrofuels means more land consumption and more use of fertilisers and herbicides. Also, the expansion of arable land comes into conflict with targets for the conservation of biodiversity. To reduce CO_2 emissions while increasing the nitrogen load and diminishing biodiversity in the process is not a sustainable path for the future.

3. Innovations often progress along predetermined paths. These are not dictated by nature but influenced by power interests and cultural patterns. The development of the automobile is a good example of this. Do we just want more economical cars, or a completely different transport model for our cities? Innovations are required for the latter, too, but would be steered in quite a different direction.

4. So far, any progress made in achieving greater efficiency, in developing renewable energies and in reducing resource consumption has

always been compensated or even overcompensated by new growth (through rebound effects).

5. Innovations are accomplished within pre-existing power structures and can reinforce these. Genetic engineering has contributed more to the proliferation of patents and the concentration of power than to boosting food production. Innovation can lead in a completely mistaken direction (exploiting new fossil sources, for instance) or pursue questionable paths (CCS, fracking). Innovations do not simply happen; they are deliberate and interest-driven.

One of the most frequently quoted sayings on the theme of "innovation" is: "The Stone Age did not end for lack of stones"; it is attributed to Sheikh Ahmed Zaki Yamani who was the Saudi Arabian oil minister from 1962 until 1986 and rose to fame at the time of the first oil price shock. The saying is wrong and misleading; it does not work for the modern age, as the Swiss author Marcel Hänggi showed in a nice deconstruction: the Sheikh is "wrong on three counts: Firstly, there was no stone lobby in the Stone Age — and no governments who could have been corrupted by it. Secondly, stones were replaced as a material for tools by metal, which was technically superior. But there is no conceivable energy source that would be technically superior to petroleum. Thirdly, and above all: Humankind has never — by a long way! — consumed as much stone as today."[166]

The same applies to other primary resources. Despite all fossil reserves, wood is still used and forests are cut down. Very rarely have we experienced the substitution of one resource with another; what we normally witness is the tapping of new sources for energy generation and resource extraction. This finding makes the Green Economy promise of uninterrupted or even accelerated growth extremely questionable. Innovation has never yet been sufficient to fulfil the promise that, in a world of finite resources, we can maintain growth — or a green variety thereof.

In this book, we have very consciously tried not to recount the general debate about growth. That debate has been argued intensively elsewhere and is ongoing. Experience teaches us that a green future with uninterrupted growth is unrealistic. We are certainly not on the path to achieving it so far. Building a strategy for the future upon an optimism about innovation that is difficult to justify seems not to be the smartest approach. Moreover, not all the problems have much to do with innovations: innovations can do little to rein in rising meat consumption; in fact, better storage and transport technologies are likely to make it expand even more. So here there is no way around a policy that promotes the idea of *less*.

Innovation, as it is understood by the majority in the Green Economy context, depends primarily on technical solutions for the central problems of humankind. In this way, the innovation concept is narrowed down and innovation is co-opted to serve productivity and growth. That is not trivial because, even at this stage, the strategies adopted dictate a certain direction. The growth-fixated concept of innovation primarily asks how *more* can be attained resource-efficiently, instead of whether we could do it *differently* and *better* with less.

The real question should be: how can we achieve a good life for all under the precondition that we leave coal, oil and gas in the ground and fundamentally reduce our absolute use of other natural resources?

Innovation can be freed from its forced wedlock with growth. Which does not mean jumping straight into new marriages with "degrowth", but asking and negotiating questions differently. Then, for example, one could discuss how urban mobility might look if it were (largely) without cars, or how transport would have to be structured if pedestrians, cyclists and public transport were given priority.

A growth-fixated concept of innovation that is aimed primarily at efficiency focuses on certain developments and tends to screen out others. That is exemplified by the Green Revolution, which is currently being invoked once again as a model. The innovations in rice cultivation set out above point to a different path for technologies. On that path, co-operations and farmers' rights, training, innovative soil management practices, and seed breeding oriented to community welfare are more important than the optimised use of high-performance varieties, chemical fertilisers and pesticides.

Simple solutions are not in sight — as the example of cement and steel demonstrates. Even low-consumption cars are constructed with steel or substitute resources, which — like aluminium — are even more energy-intensive. The crucial point is not to venture down the wrong paths. If requirements to use agrofuels are imposed, ecological problems due to land use will be exacerbated. Alternatives exist but must be debated seriously. However, some choices will be hard ones to make.

As a result of the fixation on productivity and growth, social innovations are neglected. Diverse new forms of production and consumption, mobility, housing and coexistence are being tried out in creative ways. All over the world, new spaces for thinking and action are coming into being and are fostering the development of personal initiative and responsibility for one's own lifeworld and surroundings. Beside political regulation, self-organised change processes which are supported by citizens and interconnected in networks are crucial for the transformation of the economic system, and simultaneously revitalise our democratic culture.[167]

Innovations are important but not saviours or sure-fire successes in their own right. They do not simply happen. They are a focal point of societal discourse, and society must decide which innovations it wants and which purposes innovations should serve.

PART THREE

The Green Economy's blind spots

8

A star is born – or: environmental policy in neoliberal times

When Ronald Reagan was elected President of the USA in 1981, the heyday of neoliberalism began. It was clear from the outset that this would have a powerful influence on environmental policy. Environmental policy had been founded on regulation; laws and rules had been put in place to reduce environmental degradation and bans were imposed on hazardous substances. During the 1970s, the USA (along with various other jurisdictions) had developed comprehensive legislation and court precedents around environmental issues. An impressive list of laws had been passed in the USA from the 1960s onwards, including the Clean Air Act (as early as 1963), the National Environmental Policy Act (1970), the Clean Water Act and so on. A publication of groundbreaking importance for the environmental revolution of the 1970s was the book *Silent Spring* by the American zoologist Rachel Carson. It not only poignantly highlighted the risks associated with DDT but actually resulted in practical consequences — namely the banning of DDT. Ecological critiques became politically relevant and effective. Naomi Klein once referred to the 1970s as the "golden age of environmental legislation".[168]

Under Ronald Reagan, this all changed. Environmentalists were placed under suspicion of Communism as proponents of a "command and control" approach and accused of being, in reality, intent upon centralistic planning and control over society. In voicing this indictment, the provocative Secretary of the Interior, James Watt, established an aggressive anti-environmental discourse in the conservative camp of US politics.

The swing towards neoliberalism also led important environmental organisations in the USA to change their political orientations. Instead of "sue the bastards!" and the default question "how can we stop that?" the motto became: "give people a chance to turn a profit by being smarter than the next person."[169] And so begins the story of an about-face in environmental policy — the "invention" of emissions trading. Its story is told and retold as the foundational myth of a new environmental paradigm.

Indeed, the idea initially seemed crazy. "I thought he was smoking dope", was the reaction of businessman John B. Henry when the attorney C. Boyden Gray first introduced his "cap and trade" proposal at the White House in 1980. But with vehement support from the Environmental Defense Fund (EDF), which had become an enthusiastic advocate of the new idea, in 1990 under the Bush government's Clean Air Act a "cap and trade" system was, indeed, established — i.e. a defined upper emissions limit along with tradable emissions certificates, which were to be gradually reduced in number.

How the crazy-sounding proposal could evolve into a new environmental policy paradigm in such a short time is certainly an astonishing story. The narrative reconstructed by the author and behavioural researcher, Richard Connif, also demonstrates why, in neoliberal times, "cap and trade" managed to become — as the author claims — "one of the most spectacular success stories in the history of the green movement". The idea that holds particular appeal is that "government doesn't tell polluters how to clean up their act". In one commentator's words, this would "radically disempower the regulators".[170]

Not all conservatives and corporations are enthusiastic about the idea, but as an analysis by the Massachusetts Institute of Technology (MIT)[171] attested, "cap and trade" rapidly went from being "a pariah […] to being a star".

Conniff's story of the origins of "cap and trade" traces the vital elements that made the idea so attractive to many: the flexible implementation, the great autonomy for businesses, and the alternative to the "command and control" approach. Environmental protection packaged in the logic and language of markets was thus capable of gaining majorities even in an era of economic liberalism. Over time, however, the idea of emissions trading often turned out to be more attractive than its practice. If emissions trading is tied to a "cap", an upper limit — as it must be, in order to be effective — then the setting of this limit becomes a contentious political topic and can quickly flip the enthusiasm of conservatives and entrepreneurs into scepticism or resistance. What is more, the establishment of emissions trading is bound up with a highly complex and resource-intensive regulatory system.

Be that as it may, the now very apparent difficulties of emissions trading should not blind us to the fact that principles which informed emissions trading have crept beyond such approaches to guide a mode of environmental policymaking that is informed by the Green Economy perspective.

This has consequences. It has become clear over the course of the international climate negotiations that a global climate regime with binding and ambitious reduction targets has a tough time gaining majorities. Its place is being taken by instruments and mechanisms of a power-based and growth-oriented Green Economy. From this perspective the decisive factors are technical innovations and the continuing expansion of CO_2 pricing. In the absence of one large global CO_2 market, regional markets are emerging and increasingly integrating. Apart from the evolving CO_2 pricing mechanisms, the other decisive factor is expectation. "Expectation drives innovation" is one of the key slogans. In other words — claim the proponents — there is no real need to torment the automobile industry with constant new reduction targets. Once it realises that emission-intensive cars have little or no future, then — it is argued — the industry will do the job itself by means of incentivised innovations (for electrical cars, for example). The central expectation, which the World Bank in particular never tires of proclaiming, is this: by the end of the century our world must be a net-zero-CO_2 world.

This combination of innovation, CO_2 pricing and expectation gives economic actors, especially business, not only a framework but also the longed-for freedom to service the expectations. The main thing is that neither CO_2 pricing nor innovation imposes a particular path. The market decides: "Innovation is agnostic";[172] it may not be defined by politically or ethically motivated targets but should select through success. "To meet climate and economic growth objectives in the necessary timeframe, every economy must put policy measures in place that help spur demand for clean technologies. Carbon pricing is the first critical instrument in using the power of markets to create such demand and, in the context of innovation, it has two key advantages: it is technology-neutral (letting the market decide), and it sets credible long-term perspectives."[173]

Proponents of this Green Economy option are keen to get by without political targets for the technological path and ascribe per se neutrality to technology. The economy must not be told prescriptively what is to be done, it is argued; it must retain its freedom. Politics must only frame the enabling conditions for innovation, and operate with technological neutrality.[174]

That is often overlooked by those who welcome an instrument like emissions trading for pragmatic reasons. Emissions trading, it is repeatedly heard, may not be the ideal instrument, but in the given circumstances it is the only means of establishing at least one mechanism for — albeit low — CO_2 pricing. But the emissions market is an instrument with consequences: if it is meant to be technology-neutral then it must not be disrupted by favouring or excluding particular technologies. For many advocates of CO_2 trading, one of the critical reasons that the EU Emissions Trading System (EU ETS) has "faltered" has been the establishment of parallel targets, particularly the target for increasing renewable energies. Such parallel targets do indeed have a problematic and undesirable side-effect: the successes of the "energy transition" in Germany are lowering prices on the CO_2 market.[175] At the same time, cheap CO_2 certificates are facilitating the continuing use of coal. In Germany, this results in the energy transition paradox — a growing expansion of renewable energies and a simultaneous rise in CO_2 emissions due to coal-based electricity generation. This is an absurd and absolutely unintended consequence of the energy transition. Many advocates of the CO_2 market therefore regard parallel targets — and they have a point — as a departure from the logic of the CO_2 market: industry should pursue the most cost-efficient path, without political targets. The clamour from those demanding one single target rather than parallel targets is, therefore, growing ever louder.

That this is no academic debate has been shown by the conflicts over the EU's "2030 climate & energy framework". Alongside the greenhouse gas reduction target of 40 per cent by 2030, another parallel target has been agreed for expanding the share of renewable energies, namely to 27 per cent, but that target is extremely unambitious and not binding on the national level. The rather disagreeable effect of this is that ambitious expansion of renewables in a few countries makes it possible for other countries persistently to undershoot the 27 per cent target. Antagonism towards a binding, ambitious target came particularly from the countries of the Visegrád Group[176] along with Bulgaria and Romania. In a joint declaration dated 30 September 2014, they demand: "The greenhouse gas (GHG) emissions reduction target at EU level must be set realistically and in a technology neutral way. The introduction of any legally binding renewable energy and energy efficiency targets at EU or national level is not desirable." Incidentally, this is also the position of many fossil fuel corporations in the EU, like, for example, Shell. Even though targets for energy efficiency and the expansion of renewable energies have survived as part of the EU climate and energy framework, they are becoming an increasingly minor element of European environmental policy.

What outcomes do CO_2 markets produce?

CO_2 markets cannot be an end in themselves. They must be scrutinised as to the results they deliver — even if it sometimes seems that many supporters admire the allegedly so elegant design of CO_2 markets rather than the results. The question is, does pricing operate in a manner that delivers appropriate results? How many mice is the cat catching? Can the CO_2 pricing that is emerging from emissions trading markets result in lower consumption of oil? It is perhaps unfair to point the finger at the European CO_2 market, where the CO_2 price has dropped to basement levels. But it is a plain statement of fact that the market here is not working. How about elsewhere?

Let us take a brief look at California. Its emissions trading is considered one of the great beacons of hope for better designed markets.[177] And it has done something that the EU ETS has omitted to do: since 2015 oil, and hence petrol, has been included in emissions trading. This has actually caused the petrol price to rise. To express it in litres and euros, the price at the petrol pump is now around 60 cents per litre. At that level, there is no fear yet of seeing abandoned Hummers on California's streets or surfers desperately hauling their own boards.

Petrol is an informative example. In Europe, petrol is highly taxed. This tax can be seen as another way of pricing CO_2. It is set at 65.45 cents per litre in Germany, and 61 pence per litre in the United Kingdom. If that were assumed to be the price of the CO_2 in petrol, then in Great Britain and Germany one would come up with prices of between 300 and 400 euros per tonne of CO_2.[178]

But even this quite substantial level of taxation is not capable of giving a price signal that contributes to a real transition in transportation. Worse still, as we have seen, it may not even result in more people buying low-emission vehicles. Despite a high CO_2 price, SUVs are booming.

The crucial question, in fact, is not whether CO_2 markets might be capable of delivering CO_2 pricing, but what CO_2 price we would actually need in order to achieve real changes in the economy. Economists can calculate this — or so they claim. They can inquire into the costs of avoidance of CO_2 or into price elasticity: what price do I need in order to lower demand?

In the relatively straightforward setting of Switzerland, this calculation has actually been attempted; however, it became so complex that even mainframe computers reached their limits. The rough model calculation concluded that, to influence demand effectively, it would take a price of 245 francs per tonne of CO_2.[179]

Such a price is far beyond what can be countenanced in political reality. Taking the car, for example, what would such a price mean? Were an additional CO_2 tax on this scale to take effect — i.e. on top of the taxation that already applies — then the tax burden per litre would rise to around one euro, hiking the petrol price up to two euros per litre. Certainly, this would reinforce the incentive to build fuel-efficient cars — but does that lead to less traffic, to fewer cars, to less resource consumption, to a real transition in transportation? What are the implications of that level of petrol price for the proud owner of a Porsche Cayenne who has splashed out 90,000 euros on his vehicle and would now be forced to spend an additional 500 euros per year on fuel?

Magic instead of politics?

The increasingly evident path of choice in international climate policy — technological innovation and CO_2 pricing — has never yet furnished proof of being likely to lead to a substantial drop in global CO_2 emissions — not to mention other global environmental problems. That is not intended to imply that the proposals and the policies embarked upon, particularly the establishment of CO_2 trading systems, had no impact at all. Their greatest and most momentous effect is the disempowerment of politics.

A brief look at the history of US environmental legislation shows that emissions trading came into being as a conscious counter-concept, a reaction to a strict "command and control" regulatory approach. Now the history of environmental policy — and especially of that made in Europe — cannot be reduced to a battle of market instruments against regulation, and there has never been anything like a conclusive turnaround in a particular direction. But the tireless rhetoric of the market has made its mark. Today, market-based approaches are considered modern and flexible; they are not yet preponderant at present, perhaps, but look set to become so in future. The fact that the

Magic numbers:
how to meet emissions targets
without cutting emissions

Aviation is a good example of how emissions reduction targets can be met without cutting emissions. The International Air Transport Association (IATA) has set itself targets which appear, on the face of it, to be extremely ambitious. Its vision is to achieve carbon-neutral growth (CNG) — a concept entirely in keeping with the Green Economy. The initiative's key goals are: a 1.5 per cent average annual improvement in fuel efficiency to 2020; carbon-neutral growth from 2020; and a 50 per cent absolute reduction in carbon emissions by 2050 compared with the baseline year 2020. However, with nothing but greater efficiency and even with biofuels (biokerosene), these goals are out of reach.

Is the IATA preparing for a decrease in air transport, then? Certainly not! So how can the reduction targets be achieved? In an attempt to answer that question, the air transport industry commissioned a study from Bloomberg New Energy Finance (BNEF) and the Environmental Defense Fund, an American NGO. According to Guy Turner, BNEF's Chief Economist and lead author of the report, the target will not be achieved primarily through technological innovation, but will depend on aviation being integrated into carbon trading. "This is the only way for the industry to offset its emissions."[180]

Such honesty is refreshing: from the air transport industry's perspective, the goal of carbon trading is not to reduce emissions but to offset them at an affordable price. "The analysis by Bloomberg ... showed there are enough unused, tradeable emissions allowances ... to help the aviation industry meet 30 to 50 per cent of its carbon neutral growth goal through 2050 ... the annualized cost of carbon-neutral growth ... would be ...

[up to] $4.6 bn per year … These figures … would add between $1.5 and $2 to the price of a one way fare from Paris Charles de Gaulle to New York JFK … the net cost to the aviation sector of achieving CNG2020 will be trivial."[181]

According to the IATA, this plan "keeps aviation in the fore-front of industries on managing carbon emissions".[182] At the very least, it is in the forefront in a surreal world, in which rising emissions can be sold as reductions. ■

EU ETS is the main instrument of European climate policy speaks volumes.

There are also many environmentalists who support the establish-ment and development of CO_2 trading systems as the surest course in international climate policy. What is often overlooked is that the question of *how* to bring about the agreed CO_2 reduction within a "cap and trade" system is left up to industry. Whether it is achieved with nuclear power plants, CCS or the expansion of renewable en-ergies — what counts is the measurable CO_2 reduction, and nothing else. From this perspective, state supports for the expansion of renew-able energies or the prohibition of genetically modified crops rapidly come to be viewed as competition-distorting interventions.

Among those promoting the proliferation of CO_2 markets is a lobbying group, the International Emissions Trading Association (IETA), with the neat slogan: "Climate Challenges, Market Solutions". The directory of members is revealing. Their ranks include the large petroleum groups like BP, Shell and Chevron, along with Vattenfall and Dow Chemicals and consultancy firms like KPMG. In the inter-national climate policy arena, however, not only IETA is lobbying on behalf of CO_2 markets; advocates of CCS are also increasingly repre-sented.[183]

In a world of innovations and compensations, the model of coal-fired power generation (with CCS) could also survive — and what-ever cannot be accomplished technologically will become a matter for compensation. The results are illustrated by the example of air travel. The aviation sector is not covered by the Paris Agreement. And the reduction targets, set voluntarily by the aviation industry at 50 per cent, which at first glance seem ambitious, are compatible with the probable rise in emissions. Welcome to the world of semantic dodging and confusion.

The marginalisation of politics is not a side-effect of market-based approaches but is intrinsic to them. With such approaches, it is incumbent upon politics merely to create the market—a task of the utmost complexity—and to define an overall cap on emissions, which is no small challenge, if the limit is really to have an impact.

The prioritisation of market-based instruments not only leads to a marginalisation of politics but also determines the choice of emphasis. It is not by chance that CO_2 plays a central role in the most important economic market mechanisms, for it is the most significant greenhouse gas and is therefore identified as the main factor in climate change. Hence, CO_2 has also been called the "mother of all externalities". Although it is common knowledge that the global environmental crisis is multidimensional, global environmental policy increasingly resembles a crusade—albeit often a half-hearted one—against the identified arch-enemy, CO_2. The Framework Convention on Climate Change has undeniably become the most important, if not necessarily the most successful arena of international environmental policy. In contrast, the Convention on Biological Diversity (not to mention the Convention to Combat Desertification) is largely ignored and viewed as a paper tiger.

As we have demonstrated: CO_2 is relatively easy to measure, quantify and "price"—unlike ecosystem services.[184] And it links industrial emissions with natural ecosystems (forests and peatlands) via their capacity to store CO_2 under the banner of carbon metrics. The Framework Convention on Climate Change has therefore increasingly addressed forests, and the latest thinking wishes to enlarge this to "landscapes". As a result, the Convention is tending to become a global land-use convention, meaning, land use is being integrated into emissions markets. The scale of the effect that this will have can scarcely be ascertained. Carbon therefore appears to some — in particular to the aforementioned Rachel Kyte — as the "currency of the 21st century".[185]

Such a concentration on CO_2 (or carbon) threatens to sideline other environmental issues. Agrofuels are, again and again, the best object lesson.[186] While the hype around them has subsided somewhat, the dangers are now more visible and they are seldom denied — yet the path of CO_2 storage by means of land use continues to be pursued with as much vigour as ever. A new generation of crops which facilitate more efficient use has been promised for some time now — but these, of course, also require land area and fertilisation. CO_2 pricing could make this approach to land use even more attractive, since not only fuel would be marketable but also CO_2 reduction.

Green Economy without society

Conceptions and scenarios for a Green Economy pay far too little attention to how the economy can re-embed itself into society. Questions of distribution, human rights and gender equality perspectives and democratic participation are only discussed in a perfunctory fashion, if at all. Green Economy conceptions were essentially drawn up by institutions like the OECD, the World Bank or the United Nations. The market-based instruments were developed and introduced in the framework of global UN conventions and then entered the national policy arena. None of these concepts derived from a broad, public, democratic debate based on principles of justice and human rights.

In the world of Green Economy, corporations are the most important actors. There are some good reasons for this and some that are less readily comprehensible. Corporations are considered the decisive economic "players" in this world. The green growth perspective makes no systematic provision of arenas for bargaining over the "right" path, for social actors and especially not for those who offer resistance and say "no".

Yet many key environmental policy decisions have been taken on the basis of protests and intervention by citizens. The most striking in Germany was the nuclear power phase-out. Economic and scientific arguments played an important role in the debate over nuclear power, but the ultimate deciding factor was the citizens' vote: "We do not want these nuclear power plants." The transition in energy systems is the fruit of civic commitment and of a political decision, the economic rationality of which is doubted to this day by some of the lobbies, but which is nevertheless supported by a majority of Germany's population.

All over the world, people are resisting destructive large-scale projects and claiming the freedom to say "no". This freedom need not be economically justifiable; it does not depend on opportunity costs or on the valuation of ecosystem services. It is part of the exercise of basic political choices, if the political system allows this at all. Precisely this freedom of choice tends to be undermined by the imposition of an economic frame, and torpedoed by political decisions that are not democratically legitimised and are taken in an authoritarian manner. It is then left to technology and the market to determine the course of development. With growing frequency of late, the reproach has been levelled at opponents of genetic engineering that they are responsible for global hunger and climate change, if they do not enthusiastically seize upon industry's technological solutions.

Social movements for ecological land use

One example of how greatly social movements and political actors have been able to influence environmental policy comes from Brazil. In 1988, following the death of their pioneering leader Chico Mendes, rubber-tappers succeeded in having special protected areas set up for their harvesting activity. The struggle of the rubber-tappers in Brazil garnered worldwide interest. It demonstrates an alternative to the no-human-access model of nature conservation practised in African reserves, which had long been advocated and implemented by the major international environmental organisations. In Brazil, social groups living in and from the forest stood up for the conservation of the forest, improvement of their social situation, and the safeguarding and development of their rights. The model of the rubber-tappers was adopted by other traditional communities, including in mangrove areas. In the meantime, 24 million hectares of land in the Brazilian Amazon region, an area approximately the size of former West Germany, have been designated as extractive reserves ("reservas extrativistas"). These are areas in which traditional communities have battled for and secured their rights.[187] Should this be replaced, in future, by calculations of how much the ecosystem services are "worth"?

It is often striking how little the proponents of the economic approach know about historical achievements, and how little interest they show in current social struggles. The subjective factor vanishes; all that is of interest is the rational economic actor. Not the social actors are to "save the world" but the accountants — as Pavan Sukhdev also says, albeit with a question mark.[188]

Land is a critical factor for any ecological perspective on the future. Land is not reproducible at will, and is confronted with ever new claims upon it, be it the production of crops for fuels, a constant growth in meat production, or the supply of palm oil for chocolate. As a result of new uses and a growing human race, more and more of the world's land has been converted to agricultural use or urban settlements. The share of the Earth characterised by human use is as flexible, and as subject to historical and social influences, as the entirety of its area is finite. In the last few centuries, the enlargement of agricultural and settlement areas has played out principally at the expense of forests, peatlands and swamps (today preferably described as "wetlands"). Until very recently, the conversion of forests and swamps was considered a heroic act of civilisation, and as late as 1960, the inauguration of Brasilia as the capital of Brazil was celebrated as a prize wrested from the primeval forest, with the wonderful Latin motto "urbs, ubi silva fuit" ("city where forest used to be").

In recent decades, however, this view of forests and wetlands has changed radically. They are no longer considered as barriers to civilisation but as valuable ecosystems, centres of biodiversity and CO_2 sinks. Climate change mitigation and the conservation of biodiversity are in direct conflict with strategies for the enlargement of farming and settlement areas. The conservation of forests and wetlands has become a priority of global environmental policy. Yet, in spite of all discursive appreciation of pristine forests, worldwide forest degradation continues.

An especially large blind spot: the rights of indigenous peoples

The issue is not one of a conflict between nature conservation and human use; indeed such a perception — widespread though it is — reproduces a fatal misunderstanding. The last major intact natural ecosystems in the world are usually inhabited and used by human beings. They are the habitat of indigenous peoples and traditional communities. Over time, this stock phrase has come to be used internationally to denote a multitude of human societies, which have lived in and with forests and other ecosystems, and which have relied on them for their livelihoods, for generations. Their form of use has not wrought broad-scale destruction on these ecosystems — and these are by no means small areas. For instance, in the Brazilian Amazon region alone, some 2.5 million square kilometres are designated as indigenous territories or reserves — which are predominantly used by traditional communities. That is almost five times the area of France (540,000 square kilometres). In Mexico, 80 per cent of the country's forested area is held in the traditional form of collective land tenure known as "eijidos", a type of common farmland. Worldwide it is estimated that more forest areas in the tropics are managed by indigenous peoples and traditional communities than by private owners.[189] These areas are under threat from the encroachment of commercial agriculture and forest clearance, from the exploitation of mineral deposits and from the realisation of large-scale projects like dams. The conflicts over oil in the Amazon region have attracted global attention; immense oil fields are located beneath the rainforests of

Peru and Ecuador. These are not isolated local conflicts. In Mexico, for instance, the government has granted 43,675 mining concessions in the last 15 years, which cover almost half of the country's area.[190] The German-Mexican Chamber of Commerce mentions in its advertising that 60 per cent of the country is considered to have good mining prospects.[191]

In the worldwide struggle for land, for access to natural resources and for their conservation, indigenous peoples and traditional communities hold a key position — and, for that very reason, are existentially threatened. For, despite their eminent significance, the legal status of indigenous peoples and traditional communities worldwide is very heterogeneous and often precarious. Furthermore, in the face of the interests of governments and large corporate groups, they have very little political clout. Many international efforts have therefore been targeted at improving their legal position.

Thus, in 2007 the United Nations adopted a Resolution on the Rights of Indigenous Peoples. The most important international convention for the protection of indigenous peoples is Convention 169 of the ILO (International Labour Organization of the United Nations), which grants them extensive rights to exercise an influence — including the right to say no — over development projects. To date, it is the only document valid in international law that recognises and spells out the rights of indigenous peoples. However, ILO 169 has only been ratified by 22 countries so far. Germany is not one of them.

Strengthening the much contested and imperilled rights of indigenous peoples and traditional communities could play a vital part in the preservation of remaining intact ecosystems, and hence make an important contribution to climate and biodiversity policy. Green Economy approaches disregard this, however, or treat it as a minor consideration only. Even in the UNEP conception of Green Economy, which goes the furthest in taking social aspects into account, indigenous peoples and traditional communities are not dealt with, certainly not systematically — and that is not simply a sin of omission, but a consequence of the natural capital approach. Nature as the provider of services is a natural world that is cut off from its human inhabitants. The web of life that binds humans with the rest of nature is thus unravelled. Nature without people — which scarcely exists — is made the basis for an economic construct, rather than taking the real, living relationships between humans and the rest of nature as the baseline. In other words, the economic construct of nature as natural capital desocialises nature and denaturalises humans at the same time. Given this construct, the pivotal question ceases to be the preservation of habitat and the rights of its traditional users; instead, it becomes the economic valorisation of nature as a service provider for humans.

This has very tangible and practical consequences. The centrepiece of international forest policy in recent years has been the development of the REDD mechanism. This is explicitly conceived as an economic mechanism. Rights of indigenous peoples are certainly included in REDD, but only in the "safeguards", i.e. the guidelines for the implementation of projects and programmes. Support for indigenous peoples and traditional users is linked to their economic performance, that is, they must deliver concrete, measurable results in terms of CO_2 reduction. This is the core idea of REDD.

Of course, in principle, this need not contradict a rights-based policy, but in practice the economic mechanisms have occupied the political middle ground. Green Economy is an agenda that squeezes out other approaches and alternative forms of wisdom, knowledge and practice. The overwhelmingly economic language is not without consequences: the strengthening of rights is not at the heart of the approach, including those of the actors opposing degradation — indeed, they do not even feature in Green Economy approaches. Even though — or because? — their historical track record was so very successful.

Feminist critique – not of interest?

Green Economy almost completely fails to acknowledge feminist critiques and analyses of how gender relations transform under altered economic conditions — even though the analysis of gender relations

Feminist critique of neoclassical economics

"Feminist economics analyzes the entire economy as gendered processes because the social category of gender is deeply inscribed in it as an organizing structure. The Archimedean point of feminist economics is care. Around the world, care is overwhelmingly provided by women, mostly unpaid. Neoclassical economics separates unpaid and volunteer labor for care, subsistence, and reproduction from the economy, thus making it invisible and categorizing it as unproductive and extra-economic. In contrast, feminist economics considers production and the reproductive/care economy to be interlinked and views care as adding value. The capitalist market can function only because it constantly makes use of unpaid labor for caring and for the regeneration of nature, and exploits them as 'endlessly expandable' resources. This capital-and-market-based logic of growth, increasing efficiency, and monetary accumulation contradicts the logic of care, precaution, and social security, eroding it ever more."[192] (Christa Wichterich) ■

is essential, if we want to cope with environmental crises and overcome injustice and inequality.

We need more economics, not less — that is one of the fundamental assumptions of Green Economy. This insistence on economics is targeted by current feminist critiques, including of Green Economy conceptions. A critique of the economisation of all spheres of life has crystallised from within the feminist debates. "Economics for a good life instead of for growth" is how Adelheid Biesecker puts it.[193] Also central to feminist conceptions is the idea of "caring economics" or a care economy, that is, personal, social and health care for children, young people, sick people and old people. This is part and parcel of every economy, but at the same time, it is emotional relationship work. Green Economy conceptions similarly ignore reproductive work and deny its pivotal role in every society and economy. According to Jason Moore, capitalism as a way of organising nature not only relies on "cheap nature" (unpaid costs or externalities) but equally on unpaid work (reproductive activities, often performed by women). They are not a coincidence or unintended effect of capitalism; they are rather actively produced by and a necessary co-product of capitalism.[194]

In place of the economisation of care work, feminist theorists demand societal and political appreciation of care work, and the development of social mechanisms founded on this recognition. Such a point of departure gives rise to quite different political conclusions than, for instance, pure economisation via paid work. Care work must be reorganised institutionally, societally and above all between the sexes.

A new wave of the economisation of life comes in the form of reproductive technologies. In this area there are astonishing parallels between the economisation of nature and ecosystem services and the economic valorisation of bodies and bodily substances like ova, semen and tissues, as well as the commercialisation of bodies through practices like surrogacy. Feminist critics also refer to this field of reproductive technologies as "bioeconomics".[195]

Justice – a void

Markets can do a great deal; their central place in modern economies is neither an accident nor the result of evil people or dark forces at work. Markets have proved enormously successful. They are efficient in the allocation of scarce resources — allocative efficiency is the very nucleus of success for markets — and this precise point is invoked again and again by those advocating market-based instruments in climate change mitigation and environmental protection. Although most recently — particularly in the wake of the financial crisis — doubts have been voiced about the efficiency of markets, let us leave these to one side. Markets are capable of efficiency. However, they are not suitable for creating social justice or thoroughly answering ethical questions.

Of course, there are some market-based approaches which aim to promote justice and an ethical orientation: examples are fair trade, solidarity economics or ethical investment and ethically motivated consumption. Such approaches can be important motivations for change and strengthen new actors, who then influence existing power structures. So far, however, their market share has remained extremely limited: despite appreciably climbing figures, the share of fair-trade coffee is around 2.1 per cent in Germany.[196] Another possibility is that campaigns pressing for environmental and ethical criteria can influence the choices made by businesses. But the use of sustainable palm oil in Nutella will not, by itself, prevent the expansion of palm oil production. Such approaches should never be pitted against regulation if the envisaged aim is not just "consumption with a clear conscience" but a societal and economic transformation.

The proposition that markets have nothing to do with social justice, though not entirely uncontested, is now broadly accepted. Inefficiency utterly fails to produce social justice, as bungled socialist experiments have proven all too clearly. To that extent it is perfectly reasonable to argue that efficient markets and a functioning economy provide a basis for social justice. Except that markets do not automatically help. Therefore, in all modern democracies, market mechanisms are constrained and moulded by state redistribution, by progressive taxation, by social systems and social policies, or by a minimum wage. The detailed design of these state interventions is a focal point of current political debates.

Strangely, these considerations are not prioritised highly or systematically in mainstream Green Economy thinking. If "putting a price on carbon" is to be the central steering mechanism, then there is no choice but to address the question of social justice immediately. Prices can steer allocation — particularly by encouraging the efficient management of energy and resources. Effective CO_2 pricing would — as already outlined — have immediate knock-on effects in the form of higher petrol, electricity and heating prices; and to achieve the desired effects, prices would indeed have to rise considerably. A price per litre of approximately 2.50 euros, for example, would hit many low earners hard, yet would not be a major problem for consumers with SUVs. There will surely be problems for every democratic party that commits to such a petrol price hike in its election manifesto.

We can observe the problems surrounding a socially equitable energy policy in the specific context of Germany's energy transition where the coal lobby tries to win support by complaining about high energy costs for the poor — omitting the role that fossil fuel subsidies play in this regard. Although voiced from the wrong side and for the wrong reasons, the concern is a real and important one. Germany is only slowly getting used to the concept of "energy poverty" — the concept has not even been defined unequivocally. One attempt to pin down the phenomenon measures the number of households (with low incomes) which have to spend more than ten per cent of their income on energy. This share rose from 6.4 per cent in the year 1988 to 17.8 per cent in the year 2012. The legitimation of the energy transition, as strong as it still is at present, is jeopardised by the absence of a social dimension. When it came to defining exceptions to the increased levies, obviously the (claimed) necessity to protect the competitiveness of German industry was more important than social concerns.[197]

Effective realisation of the "Put a price on carbon!" strategy would lead to substantially greater social disparities than the German energy transition. The Green Economy proposals can be searched in vain for anything resembling an answer to this question.

Nor are markets suitable for making or prejudicing normative decisions. Questions like the phasing out of nuclear power or the banning of genetically modified crops cannot be decided by the allocative efficiency of markets. These are not matters to be decided by prices, but by normative criteria. Yet, in the Green Economy, normative decisions increasingly become matters for the market — and this is precisely the consequence of the central status that is being accorded to market-based instruments.

Constrained the Green Economy options

Linking together climate policy and land use certainly is not a simple "win-win" path for climate policy. On the contrary, climate policy is rooted in eco-social conflicts, whose actors should be taken seriously. CO_2 sequestration through land use and the production of agrofuels only exacerbate — as noted — competing claims upon land use. Such conflicts are produced by the expansion of sustainable energies, too. Wind turbines have similar implications for land and resource consumption. And an electric car that runs on 100 per cent sustainably-generated energy is also built from rare minerals, requiring substances like lithium, so that it adds to the severity of resource conflicts.

However, that may not be the decisive problem at all. The struggle against catastrophic climate change may serve to delegitimise all the actors in these conflicts. Climate-related arguments are used as a new justification for large hydroelectric dams, and anyone who opposes wind turbines in their locality is immediately derided as a "nimby" ("not in my back yard"), an incorrigible egotist, who is defying the great mission of humanity. Climate policy is important, and for an energy transition we need wind turbines. But the wider diffusion of wind energy is not free of conflict. It must be open to negotiations and democratic procedures. However, in many conflicts there is a risk of climate change becoming the killer argument for quite specific ventures. The Belgian geographer Erik Swyngedouw coined the expression "the non-political politics of Climate Change" for this trend.[198]

The threat of global disaster limits political room for manoeuvre, and policy increasingly turns into the implementation of newly defined, constrained Green Economy options. The fact that the first victims are often farming families or indigenous people defending themselves against the land-grab for wind turbines, rather than the SUV drivers or frequent flyers, is nothing but a consequence of market-based mechanisms which know only one currency: CO_2. The discursive appropriation of climate change by propagandists of market solutions does actually create a "post-democratic" (Colin Crouch) or

Wind power, too, must be rights-compliant

The isthmus of Tehuantepec in southern Mexico is the only place in the Americas where there is no chain of mountains separating the Atlantic from the Pacific. Here, there is strong and constant wind, making it an ideal location for wind farms. In total, 15 are currently in operation here on the isthmus, and there are plans to increase the number to 27. Each wind farm has more than 100 turbines, and the total target installed capacity amounts to more than 10,000 MW — equivalent to five or six nuclear power plants. European firms such as Acciona, Iberdrola, ENEL, Siemens and EDF generate electricity here, mainly for corporations such as Walmart and the mining company Peñoles under power purchase agreements. More clean energy in Mexico — who could possibly object? But there is opposition from local communities, especially from smallholder farmers, who feel they are being cheated. Most wind farms are located on indigenous territories — and these communities believe they have got the raw end of the deal. "There are no jobs, there is no development, and we don't get to use the electricity. And the companies get 99 per cent of the profits," says Bettina Cruz, a local human rights activist. The rent paid for the land is ludicrously low, but the presence of wind farms means that it can no longer be used for farming, so local communities are poorer than ever. The farmers are calling for the tenancy agreements to be cancelled, but if they protest, they are branded as criminals. Many farmers are now banned from their own land. The protest groups repeatedly emphasise that they are not opposed to wind power per se but object to the conditions imposed upon them for the use of their land. As the Mexican example shows, wind power can conflict with land rights. The development of wind energy often fails to build local or regional capacities and can clash with local interests, with affected communities bearing the brunt of these major projects. In India too, according to environmental organisations, the government has set ambitious targets for renewable energy expansion but has no strategy in place to ensure that these targets are met in a democratic and equitable way. Examples like these mean that for many activists in the Global South, Green Economy is a controversial concept that can often arouse severe enmity.[199] ■

"post-political" (Chantal Mouffe) context,[200] which could scarcely be more powerful — a market that delegitimises others and legitimises itself by averting global disaster.

No alternative?

Many justifications of market-based instruments do not even resort to their supposed advantages, claiming instead simply that "there is no alternative". Nature conservation and environmental policy supposedly have their backs to the wall. Regulation or economic instruments like eco-taxes, it is claimed, are politically untenable. And the financial dire straits in nature conservation, in particular, are acutely apparent to all actors. Emissions trading therefore appears to be a politically feasible way out, and the economic valuation of ecosystem services could even turn nature conservation into a source of cash.

The appeal of such arguments is understandable. But so far the proposed mechanisms have not succeeded in delivering on their promises — and politically they lead into a pitfall, as experience with the European emissions market has shown. Instead of pondering how to revive a clinically dead emissions trading system, it should be called to mind that other instruments may be more purposeful and successful. Alternatives do exist and are realisable — but often they are politically unwanted.

The decisive challenge of climate policy is to halt the use of fossil fuels—this is increasingly becoming a consensus. Emissions trading has turned out to be a completely unfit means of achieving this particular objective. A successful approach, on the other hand—despite many problems of detail and implementation—was the German Renewable Energies Act (EEG). Under this law, economic instruments were used to subsidise an economically uncompetitive form of energy to the point where it has now become capable of generating cheap electricity. Progress like that does not come at zero cost, but at the same time, experience with the EEG demonstrates that societal majorities can be won over to support such a reconfiguration.

The fixation on emissions trading as an ostensibly flexible market instrument has suppressed the debate about other (including other economic) instruments. When discussion of a CO_2 tax flared up after the failed climate summit in Copenhagen, it was quickly choked off by pointing to the emissions trading system that did already exist. Meanwhile, Sweden's experience with that kind of tax has been positive.

Other lines of approach are equally obvious. According to IMF and IEA estimates, worldwide the unbelievable sum of around 5.3 trillion US dollars per year is still being spent on subsidies for fossil energy.[201]

Perverse incentives are not just a problem in climate policy—the conservation of nature and biodiversity also suffers from them. According to data from the German Federal Environment Agency, environmentally harmful subsidies in Germany in the year 2010 amounted to 52 billion euros. "A systematic reduction is not in prospect", the authority comments laconically. And indeed, hardly anything has changed since. Many economic policy instruments are conceivable, and are being taken up in Green Economy approaches. But why is there so little sign of implementation? Time after time, particular interests of individual branches of the economy block the change of direction towards more efficient and market-based economic activity. That is not without its irony. Subsidies are often identifiable as socially and environmentally harmful. They distort competition and make it more difficult for more resource-saving and efficient products to break into the market.

Our line of argumentation is not directed generally against economic mechanisms and instruments. It is directed against the tendency of market-based economic instruments to erode the scope for political decision making, and against the curtailment of regulation, democratic control and political alternatives, and the delegitimisation and criminalisation of protest and resistance. Certain possible courses of action and options are at risk of slipping off the political horizon completely. If emission markets and other market-based economic mechanisms become the main control panels of environmental and climate policy, there is a danger that nothing is done beside ecological refinement of growth models driven by hegemonial interests.

All the Green Economy conceptions give the economy and businesses a pivotal position as the most important actors. But *homo oeconomicus* alone will not come up with the solutions for the Great Transformation.

Civil society amid depoliticisation and shrinking spaces

The role of civil society in the debates about Green Economy is just as multifaceted and controversial as the concept of civil society itself. Civil societies assume very diverse roles and functions. For example, they can act independently of the state or on its behalf. Often they assume state functions such as social, humanitarian and environmental services, and not unusually they are kept afloat financially by state or private donors.

A committed civil society that is independent of the state can instigate social emancipatory change and perform important checking and balancing functions vis à vis governments, at national and international level. It is not for nothing that they are called the "watchdog" of state policy; they often succeed in initiating discussion of political missteps and societal issues, and they will organise political alternatives and counterpublics.

NGOs and CSOs (non-governmental and civil-society organisations) are not really the homogenous block they are frequently described as. On the contrary, they represent highly diverse causes and bring highly diverse mandates and legitimations (size of membership, internal democratic procedures of the organisation) to their involvement in political processes.

Nonetheless, one thing applies to all of them: for professional NGOs, social movements or grassroots organisations to be able to articulate positions and intervene politically, a functioning political and institutional framework is needed, including first and foremost the freedom of organisation and peaceful assembly of citizens and freedom of public expression (freedom of speech).

Beyond this, the influence and the negotiating power of NGOs and CSOs are also dependent upon the political and financial resources with which they are endowed.

Particularly in the nature conservation and environmental sector, NGOs have come into being which resemble multinational corporations, investing immense budgets in projects and bringing their influence to bear by means of lobbying. The interests such organisations represent are not always those of the indigenous population or local communities.

The example of Green Economy provides a perfect illustration of the heterogeneous and to some extent highly divergent approaches, influences and forms of intervention carried out by civil society actors. Large, primarily American but globally operating environmental organisations like Conservation International, The Nature Conservancy, the Environmental Defense Fund or WWF are, for example, very actively involved in the new market-based instruments like emissions trading, REDD and the economic valorisation of ecosystem services.

The stance taken by large environmental organisations towards many of the new technologies (e.g. CCS, geo-engineering) ranges from relatively uncritical to positively supportive. Although the positions of the individual organisations (or in some cases, different national offices or individuals within the organisations) differ considerably, one trend can be discerned in mainstream NGOs: many environmental and nature conservation organisations no longer belief in state governance. In this context, they look to market mechanisms as a promise of salvation, not only for solving problems but often also as means of replenishing their own (empty) coffers.

Where states have limited governance capacity or step into the facilitation role, they mainly resort to involving the large NGOs. In the course of multi-stakeholder rounds, rules — usually voluntary ones — are negotiated with those NGOs. Sometimes this process legitimises policies which seem rather counterproductive to the necessary trans-

REDD in Brazil

"The Guaraqueçaba Climate Action Project is a joint initiative of the U.S.-based conservation group The Nature Conservancy (TNC) and the Brazilian NGO Sociedade de Pesquisa em Vida Selvagem e Educação Ambiental (Society for Wildlife Research and Environmental Education, SPVS). The project is located in the coastal municipalities of Antonina and Guaraqueçaba, in the state of Paraná. Three of the world's largest carbon emitters—General Motors (GM), American Electric Power and Texaco/Chevron—provided the funding for TNC's Brazilian partner SPVS to buy 19,000 hectares of land, mostly from cattle ranchers who held land but did not live in the region. The land bought with the money from the three corporations had been degraded by water buffalo grazing and was to be restored as part of the forest carbon project. The carbon absorbed and saved in the vegetation as a result of project activities was to provide carbon credits to the corporate funders of the project. [...] The Guaraqueçaba region is home to one of the few remaining intact and largely non-fragmented areas of Mata Atlântica, or Atlantic Forest, in Brazil. It is also home to approximately 10,000 people, of whom 1,700 live in the town of Guaraqueçaba. Even though their way of life is dependent on the forests and mangroves, registering or fencing off the land they depended on was never considered necessary by the Caiçara communities: the territory was understood as an area of shared use, belonging to everyone. Most of the land in the area was legally classified as *terra devoluta*, publicly owned land on which the families lived with their belongings that were passed down from generation to generation. They worked the land and forest, sometimes individually as a family unit, sometimes collectively. [...] What the companies own is [...] not the land, or the trees, or even the carbon in the trees, but the right during the 40-year duration of the project to use a portion of the carbon stored in the trees as compensation for their carbon dioxide emissions, through the carbon credits they receive. Indirectly, therefore, they influence how the land that generates the carbon credits is used. [...] In sharp contrast with the benefits and employment that SPVS and TNC promised, Caiçara communities connect the Guaraqueçaba Climate Action Project with persecution by the Força Verde and harassment, violations of human rights, including social, cultural and environmental rights, and the loss of access to the forests that have always provided for them."[202] (Jutta Kill) ▪

formation, and which are enacted without providing for accountability or democratic feedback loops regarding the people affected and their democratically legitimised stakeholder representatives or grassroots social movements. There are numerous examples of how such processes can undermine local resistance (against deforestation, for example). The result is often a depoliticisation or division of civil society. One such example is the Roundtable on Sustainable Palm Oil (RSPO), founded in 2004 on the initiative of WWF. It attempts to promote sustainable production methods for palm oil. Apart from environmental conservation organisations and other NGOs, the members are principally businesses (plantation operators, traders and industrial purchasers of palm oil as well as investors and banks). More than 250 environmental, social and human rights NGOs around the globe criticise the Roundtable as a greenwashing platform and a fraud.[203]

Shrinking and closing spaces

In addition to these forms of co-optation, there is another, very different and unsettling trend. We are currently seeing a wave of legal, bureaucratic and tax measures which massively restrict the activities of civil society, particularly of NGOs. These are targeted not only at national NGOs but especially at foreign organisations and foundations providing support to partners. In some countries, full-bodied agitation and defamation campaigns are mounted against any form of opposition. NGOs and critical minds are decried, if they co-operate with foreign organisations or foundations, as "the long arm" of foreign influence or as "foreign agents". Every form of restriction seems permissible: activists are arrested, accounts frozen, threats uttered, licences withdrawn, websites blocked, offices closed, registrations compelled. In many countries, internal security and the battle against terrorism is an acceptable pretext for gagging or prohibiting democratic organisations — exploiting a climate of suspicion to legitimise all repressive measures.

In democratic or partially democratic countries, we increasingly observe that entire packages of measures by governments are directed primarily against social movements and NGOs, which are organising opposition to large-scale projects like coal, oil or gas exploitation and other infrastructure and investment projects (for example, pipelines or land grabbing).

However, it is not only in China, Russia, India, Ethiopia, Turkey or Cambodia that environmentalists come under pressure as a part of civil society. Wherever control over the access to and exploitation of strategic natural resources is an issue — from coal, oil and gas to water, forests, land and biodiversity, and ultimately genetic resources — those in power reach for flexible strategies in order to secure their own power and the survival of their business model. This phenomenon was noted by Maina Kiai, United Nations Special Rapporteur on the rights to freedom of peaceful assembly and of organisation, in his reports. In addition to cases from developing countries, he also describes cases of human rights violations relating to resource issues in Canada and Australia.[204]

Murders of activists (particularly those involved in local resistance) are becoming more frequent. The British NGO Global Witness states in its report "How Many More?"[205] that the number of environmental activists killed is steadily increasing. The global total in the year 2014 was 116—which is approximately two murders per week. The most dangerous country for environmental activists is Honduras, with 101 deaths between 2010 and 2014. A prominent victim in March 2016 was Berta Cáceres, who was murdered in her house for opposing a hydroelectric project. And those are just the known cases. The number of unreported cases is presumably much higher, since the murders often take place in remote regions.

Global Witness presumes the cause to be the increased pressure on and conflicts over natural resources like land or mineral and fossil resources. Those who end up in the firing line are those who question power and control (for example over natural resources), expose corruption and injustice and refuse to be integrated into voluntary initiatives of industry, but wish to expose and call a halt to its political influence. In many cases, this is not a structured civil society organised by means of NGOs but a multifaceted local resistance movement which, lacking international visibility or a high profile, has all the more difficulty protecting itself from repression.

Worldwide, there are around 60 NGO laws which massively inhibit the freedom of NGOs and civil society to take action. The number and severity of such laws are on the increase. The core concern of the new NGO laws is well as older ones currently being modified is to cut off national organisations from foreign funding or to bring these funding flows under state control. A particular means used to restrict freedom of action and to intimidate NGOs are the rules on registration and the regulations on obligatory reporting. The Russian NGO law has gained notoriety and imitators (e.g. in Malaysia and in the Israeli draft law). Anyone who receives money from abroad must undergo registration as a "foreign agent". The designation "agent" is not only found in NGO laws. Labelling critical thinkers and actors as "Western agents" is a popular move in defamation campaigns—whether in Venezuela, Egypt, Ecuador or Russia.

In autocratic countries, the foremost objective is to nip any form of organisation or public protest in the bud. The NGO laws are not the only legislative measures which inhibit civil society's freedom of action: security laws, antiterrorism laws, media laws—all of these contain restrictions on the capacity for action of civil society actors, social movements, journalists, lawyers, bloggers and critical professional associations.

In many countries, governments are concerned both to keep claims to democratic participation at bay and suppress protests against the "development model". Any criticism, any questioning of the elites' political and economic power is stifled from the outset by all available means. These governments' fear of protest and of the will of their citizens appears to be immense. Loss of political power is the major threat; all too often, defence against that goes hand in hand with securing economic interests. Protests against land grabs and large-scale projects "are not welcome". "Outside" financing is a convenient pretext used to stoke overtly nationalistic resentments as a diversion from these interests. Garcia Linera, the Vice President of Bolivia denounced national think tanks and NGOs as representatives of the "imperial environmental discourse". The revocation of Greenpeace India's license is interpreted as a declaration of war by the Indian government upon all organisations that oppose the Indian development and growth model. Cutting off national activists from external funding flows and digital connections is one approach; criminal prosecution and secret service surveillance in their own country is another; the combination of both not only narrows the scope for action, but can stifle it altogether.

The aim of repressive practices and new laws is to gag every critical voice that is raised against government action or corporate interests. Civil society involvement is nevertheless still allowed, if it is non-political and continues to assume state functions, e.g. in the social and in the environmental sector, without advancing claims for democratic participation or addressing structural causes of poverty and environmental degradation. Depoliticised NGOs are welcome and may accept foreign money, albeit under reinforced state control. The division into *good* and *bad* or *anti-state* NGOs has been in full swing for a long time, and the many new NGO laws are "legalising" this ongoing process.

Western NGOs, foundations and think tanks are increasingly placing the theme of shrinking and closing spaces on the political agenda. That is a good thing. Political answers are anything but simple because fundamental human rights like freedom of organisation, peaceful association and free speech, as adopted by the United Nations member states in the 1948 Universal Declaration of Human Rights, are sacrificed far too often on the altar of economic, foreign and security policy interests of governments. Without democratic freedoms and processes, there will be no social and ecological transformation and adaptation in the global South, East and West except for very limited processes within authoritarian structures. For us, however, democratic participation and human rights are inseparably linked with policies for the mitigation of climate change and conservation of ecosystems and livelihoods.

Conclusion:
making the case
for a new Political Ecology

———

Now, more than ever, we possess intricate knowledge about the inter-play within geo-ecological systems and the consequences of human interventions. Climatologists and environmental scientists are in agreement: we are already exceeding biophysical limits, with irrevers-ible consequences for the biosphere and the future of humankind as a whole. That is not alarmism but a summoning call to respond to this knowledge and set ambitious limits upon emissions of all kinds as well as on resource consumption. This is a political task of the first order. It is an ethical question how we distribute the remaining eco-logical space fairly and equitably for present and future generations, assuming that good living, freedom and justice for all people on Earth are to remain a political goal. And it must remain a goal.

How encompassing and far-reaching does this transformation need to be, though? And which conceptions and which political, tech-nological, social and cultural innovations will let us realise it? What does an economy that stays within the planetary boundaries look like? And how can we transform the present capitalist mode of produc-tion and consumption so as not to precipitate a collapse resulting in uncontrollable social and political rifts? We are only just beginning to find answers; but a host of investigations are under way, which form the starting point and the framework for controversies and disputes.

We have elucidated and questioned the hypotheses and the prac-tice of Green Economy from a discourse-critical and power-critical standpoint. It is widely understood that we need radical steps for a global transformation. However, it is highly contentious, how quickly we should change course, and with which political interventions and which technologies.

Therefore, the foremost task of an ecological project for the future is to mobilise politically for the essential transformation and to develop concepts for new modes of production and economic activity. Continuing the project of the modern era means: combining the vision of democratic participation and an end to poverty and injustice with the latest knowledge about the planetary boundaries.

Transformation as a political task includes highlighting where this path is likely to run into conflicts. Particularly the most recent history of Green Economy is full of trade-offs. These manifest themselves clearly — as we have outlined — with regard to agrofuels. Even in the case of win-win solutions, goal conflicts must be acknowledged and made transparent at an early stage. The social and ecological consequences of new technologies and productions need to be widely discussed in society. For a radical change of course does not happen without conflicts and ruptures. Political decision-makers on all levels are afraid of this fact; parties fear election losses and many professional non-governmental organisations, for the sake of their donation revenues, prefer to espouse simple solutions rather than complexity.

To suggest that more (green) economics is the path out of crisis and that we will be saved by technological innovations and new market mechanisms may well be counter-productive for political mobilisation. Minimising and sugarcoating do not help; nor does paralysis-inducing resignation. Breaking people down into optimists and pessimists, or into traditionalists and modernisers, which is unfortunately a common tactic in environmental and social debates, is nonsensical as well as unhelpful. It only distracts from the size of the challenge of a radical transformation, which requires all of society's creative minds — in institutions, in politics and the economy — for the process of rethinking and changing course.

All the same, there is something like a common bond among the many people in politics, the economy and society who know that we must depart from the current business and production model. This consensus offers a major opportunity for a successful exit from fossil energies — the "brown agenda" — with its social and environmental depredations. Here, the potentials to forge strong political alliances are far from having been exhausted.

Another consensus is that by using new and more efficient technologies, we can at least gain time. However, we must face up more explicitly to the political fact that, despite these consensuses, there may still be huge disagreements over the deeper causes of socio-ecological crises and, hence, also over the ways forward and the ultimate goals. To acknowledge these differences of opinion and seek to debate them whilst continuing to forge alliances for preliminary steps, even if there is not consensus on all questions, should be the principle informing the culture of political debate in the complicated search for the new and transformative.

We argue for a re-politicisation of ecology, which acknowledges the scientific findings about the biophysical limits of our planet and which therefore endorses a radical transformation, whilst facing up to the questions of justice and power. Every vision of prosperity for all the Earth's citizens must come to grips with the following questions: whom does nature belong to? Who has access, who controls the resources, and how do we distribute them among ourselves?

We make the case for taking up the concept of Political Ecology once again, without dealing in detail here with the discourse and the "intellectual product of the 1970s" and its ideological ballast.[206] This concept attempts to capture the complex relationship of politics and ecology, the human–nature relationship. Today from the perspective of planetary boundaries and global climate and resource equity, the question of how to radically reverse the trend is becoming ever more acute. In this context, Political Ecology turns to discourses critical of power and capitalism.

Political Ecology encompasses a reform policy which leaves some freedom of action for the future and buys time to complete the quest for more comprehensive transformation. There are a vast number of realisable reform options for the energy, agricultural and transport transition, for environmental urban planning and much more. Equally there are realisable reform proposals for an alternative, equitable and environmentally sustainable finance, trade and investment policy. We know the regulatory policy instruments that are capable of limiting emissions and resource consumption. And we know how we can steer processes to bring about democratisation of asset accumulation and more equitable redistribution within societies and between the sexes. Countless such proposals, initiatives and campaigns do not fail because there are no alternatives, but because of political and economic power structures.

For that precise reason we are under an urgent imperative to limit and curtail the concentration of economic power. However, this is either not happening, or not to the extent necessary. All too often, politics lays itself open to blackmail, or bows to the lobbies instead of informing society and fighting to convince majorities. Apart from limiting, containing and redistributing power, environmental policy should concentrate once more on regulatory policy instruments for climate change mitigation or biodiversity conservation — these were very successful with thresholds, bans and other politically-set incentives — instead of forcing a further economisation of nature and relying primarily on market-based instruments. The abolition of environmentally and socially harmful subsidies running into billions should also be put on the political agenda at last — nationally and multilaterally. That, too, is a power issue because the subsidies are predominantly of benefit to elites. In all Green Economy scenarios there is at least a broad consensus on the theme of subsidies.

What is therefore needed is a regulating state, under democratic control, which is committed to public welfare and ecological provision for the future, as well as a robust civil society capable of dealing with conflict. To achieve that alone is a Herculean task, for states, state institutions and civil society actors (from trade unions to professional non-governmental organisations) are themselves part of a growth imperative and addressees of powerfully influential lobbies — from businesses to certain trade unions.

Governments — be they democratic or not — are now more than ever creating framework conditions that facilitate capital utilisation, favourable investment conditions and consumerism. The democracies at least are torn two ways in that, aside from the welfare promise, they must also provide or protect public goods such as a healthy environment, education, liberty and human rights. This is also part of their political legitimation, which is why democratic systems, parliamentary and non-parliamentary as well as other democratic processes and procedures have a greater chance of furthering the breakthrough of a social and ecological transformation agenda if corresponding societal majorities can be mobilised (as was the case with nuclear power phase-out, the energy transition and bans on genetic engineering).

That, too, will involve conflict. It is an illusion to believe that technical progress can render such conflicts superfluous. Power structures leave their traces on technical progress, and decisions about which technological developments we do and do not want must remain a part of political decision making and democratic debate.

"The peculiarity of modern democracy resides in the acknowledgement and legitimisation of conflict and in the refusal to suppress it by imposing an authoritarian order."[207] Those were the words of Chantal Mouffe, who analysed how conflict has been and continues to be edged out from the political agenda in favour of consensus-oriented procedures. She rightly considers differences of opinion and conflicts in a pluralistic democracy to be not only legitimate, but necessary. "They contain the stuff of which democratic policy is made."[208]

Politics — and Political Ecology — needs exactly that: more courage to tolerate conflict and confrontation. The necessary turnaround has not been accomplished in pressing financial market regulation; nor have important spheres of production been decarbonised and dematerialised.

"How worthwhile is an economic system which makes us destroy our ecological life-support base, which presents us with repeated financial crises and which shreds our societies thanks to growing inequality?" asks the German Green MEP Gerhard Schick.[209] He calls for an economy that serves the people and not the other way round. Political Ecology can thus come together with a Green Economy that actually merits the name.

Political Ecology, as we understand it, refers to the existing power relations between North and South, between rich and poor, and between men and women. If we want to organise an exit from the brown, resource-devouring economy, we must properly understand the economic and political interests and power resources of those who desire hegemony via the path of transformation. Yet another aspect of a green transformation paradigm in line with Political Ecology principles is the art of abstinence, contraction, reduction. The question of sufficiency, "how much is enough?", cannot be avoided, certainly not in the context of global justice. The protagonists of the Green Economy mainstream do not want to hear anything about it. It does not fit into the "business model".

The great transformation will not succeed without tough negotiation, conflict and resistance. A complete reconciliation of economics and politics will not be possible, and certainly not through new price mechanisms alone. On the contrary: Political Ecology deals specifically with the fact that far-reaching societal changes and upheavals will not happen without social and ecological struggles. In some circumstances, these are even the essence and the nucleus of change. We must conceive of consensus, dispute and conflict as part of the transformation, as part of the necessary quest that we are embarking upon. For that we need to strengthen the autonomy of the political, and not subordinate it to the economic, by whatever "green" credentials it is legitimised.

Civil society organisations are given great weight in the design and realisation of the socio-ecological transformation. However, on the one hand, their effectiveness is hopelessly overestimated: in general (apart from a few large foundations and conservation organisations) they are not equipped with the same resources as the large business lobbies; and ultimately they are not decision-makers but can only influence political decisions, at the most. And on the other hand, they are part of a consensus machine that seeks dialogue more than conflict. While this often works well for them, it is not unusual for them to be co-opted. In our understanding of Political Ecology, many NGOs are not at all interested in major structural changes or in questions of power and distribution. Ultimately, in many countries around the world, actors who enter into conflicts, point out iniquity and get involved in campaigning for a more equitable world, ecologically and socially, are increasingly placed under suspicion and subjected to massive repression.

We conclude our arguments for a new Political Ecology with the wish for even more civil society organisations to dedicate themselves to social and environmental transformation, and alongside their numerous and frequently consensus-oriented activities, also to choose more radical forms of intervention or forge alliances with other more radical (and grassroots) organisations and movements and agree on a strategic division of labour.

The alliances in Germany, Europe and worldwide against the Transatlantic Trade and Investment Partnership (TTIP), the global anti-coal and anti-fracking campaigns and the global movement for agroecology are models that offer encouragement.

What those who suffer from political exclusion, repression, violence and criminalisation need, more urgently than ever, is our political solidarity and the intervention of democratic governments to urge respect for basic human rights, which include the freedom of peaceful assembly, freedom of organisation, free speech and freedom of opinion. For freedom, justice, human rights, diversity and democratic principles are the normative foundation upon which transformative strategies will be negotiated for a liveable future.

Notes

1 http://www.boell.de/en/2015/12/15/cop-21-and-paris-agreement-force-awakened

2 Carbon Metrics – Global abstractions and ecological epistemicide. An essay by Camila Moreno, Daniel Speich Chassé and Lili Fuhr, volume 42 of the Publication Series Ecology. Edited by the Heinrich Böll Foundation, 2015

3 More about this at: http://www.stockholmresilience.org/21/research/research-programmes/planetary-boundaries.html. Update 2015: http://www.stockholmresilience.org/21/research/research-programmes/planetary-boundaries/planetary-boundaries-data.html. The updated version 2015 is available here: http://www.sciencemag.org/content/347/6223/1259855.full (registration necessary).

4 See e.g., Markus Wissen (2014): The political ecology of agrofuels: conceptual remarks, in: Dietz, Kristina, et al. (eds): The Political Ecology of Agrofuels, Abingdon, pp. 16–33

5 WBGU (2011): World in Transition – A Social Contract for Sustainability, Berlin, p. 25

6 OECD (2011): Towards Green Growth, May 2011, OECD

7 www.boell.de/en/coalatlas

8 https://www.foeeurope.org/tar-sands

9 Robert Howarth: Methane emissions and climatic warming risk from hydraulic fracturing and shale gas development: implications for policy (https://www.dovepress.com/methane-emissions-and-climatic-warming-risk-from-hydraulic-fracturing--peer-reviewed-fulltext-article-EECT), published 8 October 2015

10 Currently indications are mounting that a temperature rise of 2 degrees Celsius above the pre-industrial level is already far too much, and the threshold for even half-way manageable catastrophic climate change must be set far lower—for example, at 1.5 degrees, which has now been set as a new global goal post with the Paris Agreement. Just a few months before the 2015 climate summit in Paris, for example, the renowned climate scientist James Hansen published a study on sea-level rise, written collaboratively with other scientists. The disturbing facts: according to the study we must gear up for several metres of sea-level rise in the coming 50 years, as well as devastating storms. That is far above the assumptions made in the IPCC's latest Assessment Report on the state of knowledge on climate change. (The study by James Hansen can be found at http://www.atmos-chem-phys-discuss.net).

11 http://www.carbontracker.org/report/carbon-bubble/

12 Christophe McGlade, Paul Ekins (2015): "The geographical distribution of fossil fuels unused when limiting global warming to 2 °C". In: *Nature* 517, pp. 187–190 (8 January 2015)

13 "Global Warming's Terrifying New Math". *Rolling Stone*, August 2012; http://www.rollingstone.com/politics/news/global-warmings-terrifying-new-math-20120719?page=2

14 The variations in figures derive primarily from the fact that the institutions assume different probabilities of achieving the 2°C goal.

15 This concerns a few states like former Soviet republics, China, Poland, or North Korea, which have directly extracted or are directly extracting.

16 Cf. http://www.climateaccountability.org/

17 Cf. http://carbonmajors.org/

18 "The fossil fuel bailout: G20 subsidies for oil gas and coal exploration"; http://priceofoil.org/content/uploads/2014/11/G20-Fossil-Fuel-Bailout-Full.pdf

19 Cf. http://kochcash.org/

20 www.carbonmajors.org

21 www.boell.de/en/coalatlas

22 https://www.iea.org/publications/freepublications/publication/WEO2015SpecialReportonEnergyandClimateChange.pdf

23 www.boell.de/en/coalatlas

24 Cf. http://www.ewea.org/fileadmin/files/library/publications/statistics/EWEA Annual-Statistics-2014.pdf, p. 3

25 These are rather conservative estimates; on the latest state of research: http://www.sciencemag.org/content/344/6187/1246752.abstract

26 Cf. Living Planet Report 2014: assets.panda.org/downloads/wwf_lpr2014_low_res.pdf

27 Cf. http://www.spiegel.de/wissenschaft/natur/satellitenfotos-zeigen-immer schnellere-regenwald-abholzung-a-1020637.html

28 Cf. http://www.fr-online.de/natur/inventur-der-natur-fuer-tiere-wird-s-langsam-eng,5028038,26670426.html. This contains a good overview of the report.

29 A good survey (in German) can be found at: http://www.bodenwelten.de/content/flächenverbrauch-trends-und-entwicklungen

30 Umweltbundesamt (2013): Sustainable use of Global Land and Biomass Resources, Dessau; https://www.umweltbundesamt.de/en/publikationen/sustainable-use-of-global-land-biomass-resources

31 UNEP (2014): Assessing Global Land Use: Balancing Consumption with Sustainable Supply. A Report of the Working Group on Land and Soils of the International Resource Panel; http://www.unep.org/resourcepanel-old/Portals/24102/PDFs//Full_Report-Assessing_Global_Land_UseEnglish_(PDF).pdf

32 WBGU (2011), p. 131

33 See generally on this topic: Heinrich-Böll-Stiftung et al. (Eds) (2015): Soil Atlas. Facts and figures about earth, land and fields, Berlin

34 https://www.bmz.de/en/publications/archiv/type_of_publication/strategies/Strategiepapier321_02_2012.pdf

35 Uwe Hoering (2015): "Im Griff der Konzerne", in: Inkota Dossier: Private Konzerne in der Landwirtschaft, Berlin

36 https://www.evb.ch/fileadmin/files/documents/Shop/EvB_Agropoly_DE_Neu auflage_2014_140707.pdf

37 http://www.etcgroup.org/content/breaking-bad-big-ag-mega-mergers-play

38 http://www.etcgroup.org/content/breaking-bad-big-ag-mega-mergers-play

39 J. Pretty et al. (2006): "Resource-conserving agriculture increases yields in developing countries", in: *Environmental Science & Technology* 3(1), pp. 24–43

40 IAASTD (2009): International Assessment of Agricultural Knowledge Science and Technology for Development, Agriculture at Crossroads, Global Report, Washington, DC

41 Cf. http://elibrary.worldbank.org

42 Brand and Wissen coined the term "imperial mode of living", by which they mean a way of life that is not generalisable in view of the ecological boundaries, and is ultimately based on the exclusion of large parts of the world population from a lifestyle promulgated in the "rich" countries. More on this (in German) here: Ulrich Brand, Markus Wissen (2013): Imperiale Lebensweise. E-reader: http://www.buko.info/fileadmin/user_upload/doc/reader/BUKO-Gesnat-Seminar-04-2013-Reader-V1.pdf

43 Oxfam (2014): Even it up – Time to End Extreme Inequality, Oxford, p. 8. Lucas Chancel and Thomas Piketty (2015): Carbon and inequaliy: from Kyoto to Paris. http://piketty.pse.ens.fr/files/ChancelPiketty2015.pdf

44 Cf. Oxfam: "An Economy For the 1%: How privilege and power in the economy drive extreme inequality and how this can be stopped", January 2016 (http://oxfamilibrary.openrepository.com/oxfam/bitstream/10546/592643/39/bp210-economy-one-percent-tax-havens-180116-en.pdf)

45 Cf. Global Wealth Data Book, p. 116, https://publications.credit-suisse.com/tasks/render/file/?fileID=5521F296-D460-2B88-081889DB12817E02

46 Cf. Soil Atlas, loc. cit., figure p. 26

47 Cf. http://www.welthungerhilfe.de/en/about-us/media-centre/artikel/mediathek/global-hunger-index-2014.html

48 A good overview of the debate (in German) is provided in: http://www.zeit.de/2014/07/szenarioschrumpfende-weltbevoelkerung

49 See http://esa.un.org/unpd/wpp/unpp/panel_population.htm

50 See http://www.kateraworth.com/doughnut/

51 Molly Scott Cato (2008): Green Economics: An Introduction to Theory, Policy and Practice, London, p. 5

52 Jane Glesson-White (2014): Six Capitals, New York, p. 132

53 This quote from Pavan Sukhdev is from a TED talk he gave: https://www.ted.com/talks/pavan_sukhdev_what_s_the_price_of_nature#t-208984

54 UNEP (2011): Towards a Green Economy: Pathways to Sustainable Development and Poverty Eradication, p. 16, www.unep.org/greeneconomy

55 See http://www.businessgreen.com/bg/news/2173713/world-bank-calls-countries-urgent-steps-protect-natural-capital

56 Michael Jacobs provides a good overview of the "Green Economy" and "Green Growth" concepts: Michael Jacobs (2012): Green Growth: Economic Theory and Political Discourse, Grantham Research Institute on Climate Change and the Environment, Working Paper 92. See page 3 here: http://www.unep.org/greeneconomy/Portals/88/documents/partnerships/GGKP%20Moving%20towards%20a%20Common%20Approach%20on%20Green%20Growth%20Indicators.pdf

57 See http://new.unep.org/greeneconomy/Portals/88/documents/partnerships/ GGKP%20Moving%20towards%20a%20Common%20Approach%20on%20 Green%20Growth%20Indicators.pdf, p. 3

58 See BMBF: Green Economy Research Agenda, p. 10, https://www.bmbf.de/pub/ Green_Economy_Research_Agenda.pdf

59 There was a second New Climate Economy Report in the year 2015. Both reports can be found here: http://newclimateeconomy.report/

60 The quote is found, for example, in this interview with Sukhdev: http://e360.yale. edu/feature/putting_a_price_on_the_real_value_of_nature/2481/

61 World Bank (2012): Inclusive Green Growth, Washington, DC, p. 45, http:// siteresources.worldbank.org/EXTSDNET/Resources/Inclusive_Green_Growth_ May_2012.pdf

62 Cf.: http://www.theguardian.com/environment/2012/may/09/world-bankurgent-natural-capital

63 See: Robert Costanza: Natural capital, http://www.eoearth.org/view/article/ 154791/

64 World Bank (2012), loc. cit., p. 105

65 In the practice of natural capital valuation, there is a blurring of precisely this distinction between "stocks", the actual natural assets or resources, and "flows", the ecosystem services deriving from them; an untidiness that the founder of "Ecological Economics", Herman Daly, repeatedly laments.

66 See: http://www.ey.com

67 See: http://www.naturalcapitalcoalition.org/why-natural-capital.html

68 See: http://www.envplan.com/abstract.cgi?id=d3304

69 See: http://unstats.un.org/unsd/envaccounting/eea_white_cover.pdf

70 See: http://unstats.un.org/unsd/envaccounting/White_cover.pdf, p. 1

71 Two recent studies by UNEP and WWF give and good and detailed insight into the "natural capital accounting" approach; cf.: http://www.unep-wcmc.org/system/ dataset_file_fields/files/000/000/232/original/NCR-LR_Mixed.pdf?1406906252 und http://d2ouvy59p0dg6k.cloudfront.net/downloads/background_accounting_ for_natural_capital_in_eu_policy_decision_making_final.pdf

72 See: http://www.theguardian.com/environment/georgemonbiot/2014/jul/24/ price-nature-neoliberal-capital-road-ruin

73 See: http://www.theguardian.com/sustainable-business/natural-capital-neoliberal-road-ruin-george-monbiot-experts-debate. All the following quotes are taken from here.

74 See: Robert Costanza: Natural capital, http://www.eoearth.org/view/article/ 154791/

75 More on this debate: http://www.greattransition.org/publication/monetizing-nature-taking-precaution-on-a-slippery-slope

76 This and the following quote are taken from here: http://steadystate.org/use-and-abuse-of-thenatural-capital-concept/

77 http://www.nachhaltigkeit.info/artikel/carbon_disclosure_project_cdp_1622. htm

78 World Bank Group (2014): State and Trends of Carbon Pricing, Washington, DC, p. 15, http://www.wds.worldbank.org

79 https://www.boell.de/sites/default/files/2015-11-09_carbon_metrics.pdf

80 The CDM Methodology Booklet gives an insight into the complexity of the methods developed: https://cdm.unfccc.int/methodologies/documentation/1411/CDM-Methodology-Booklet_fullversion_PART_1.pdf

81 "But REDD+ has its limitations too, the biggest being that it 'will never be able to generate enough financial support to equal the opportunity cost of deforestation in some areas and for some crops,' according to Meyer." http://news.mongabay.com/2015/09/an-alternative-to-help-companies-fulfill-zero-deforestation-pledges/

82 Conflicts in REDD projects have been very well documented in the meantime. For instance the Center for International Forestry Research (CIFOR) has published a study under the title "Redd on the Ground". Although CIFOR belongs to the REDD protagonists, the balance sheet of the study is sobering. The study can be viewed here: http://www.cifor.org/publications/pdf_files/books/BCIFOR1403.pdf. – In a study looking at 25 REDD projects, Jutta Kill comes to the following conclusion: "The local (and often indigenous) population which lives in the forest regions concerned is seldom asked if it actually wants any such project. Instead of addressing the causes of deforestation (namely industrialised agriculture, for example), the indigenous forest users are singled out as a disruptive factor. A CO_2-certificates regime (which does not privatise the forest as such, but transforms an 'ecosystem service'—namely the CO_2 storage capacity of biomass—into a tradeable commodity) undermines fundamental human rights, leads to social conflicts (e.g. over the distribution of revenues from trading) and ultimately contributes little to mitigating climate change." (Cf.: http://www.deutscheklima finanzierung.de/blog/2015/03/konflikte-widerspruche-und-lugen-rund-um-redd/.) The study can be viewed here: http://wrm.org.uy/wp-content/uploads/2014/12/REDD-A-Collection-of-Conflict_Contradictions_Lies_expanded.pdf

83 "Up to 50% of the EU-wide reductions over the period 2008-2020 can be achieved by buying CDM and JI offsets: approximately 1.6 billion credits. The EU-ETS is the largest offset buyer to date." See: http://carbonmarketwatch.org/category/eu-climate-policy/eu-ets/

84 See: http://www.sacbee.com/opinion/op-ed/soapbox/article4453841.html#story link=cpy

85 Quoted after: http://www.worldbank.org/en/news/speech/2014/12/08/transform ing-the-economy-to-achieve-zero-net-emissions

86 Cf.: http://www.project-syndicate.org/commentary/net-zero-emissions-notenough-by-lili-fuhr-and-niclas-h-llstr-m-2014-12/german#fb0KIiGtGJcMVDeP.99

87 See: http://blogs.worldbank.org/climatechange/get-net-zero-emissions-we-need healthy-landscapes

88 "Although the 1.5 degree goal is hailed as one of the major successes of COP21, it holds a certain irony, in that it will likely require significant areas of land for carbon sequestration and an unknown quantity of potentially dangerous negative emissions technologies, all which must be balanced with food security, the safety and rights of people, biodiversity conservation, and the new global adaptation goal. The world will walk a delicate line on these issues and will require transformational change in terms of national cross-sectoral coordination in many countries." (Stephen Leonard, CIFOR, http://blog.cifor.org/38995/paris-agreement-not-perfect-but-the-best-we-could-get?fnl=en)

89   Quoted passage translated from the German for convenience. See: http://www.
     bmz.de/de/was_wir_machen/themen/umwelt/biodiversitaet/arbeitsfelder/
     neue_ansaetze/

90   Ibid.

91   Cf.: http://rosalux-europa.info/publications/books/economic-valuation-of-
     nature/

92   A good overview is found in Pirard and Lapeyre: http://www.cifor.org/publica
     tions/pdf_files/articles/APirard1402.pdf

93   Cf.: http://www.academia.edu/3634305/Market_mechanism_or_subsidy_in_dis
     guise_Governing_payment_for_environmental_services_in_Costa_Rica_with_
     Robert_Fletcher_

94   On this: http://www.umb.no/statisk/noragric/publications/reports/2011_nor_
     rep_60.pdf

95   To cite just one example: "The lack of prices and property rights associated with
     ecosystem services has resulted in externalities in which uncompensated or non-
     agreed costs are imposed on nature. The negative impacts on biodiversity and
     ecosystems from such externalities are severe and rapidly escalating." Accord-
     ing to WWF: http://d2ouvy59p0dg6k.cloudfront.net/downloads/background_
     accounting_for_natural_capital_in_eu_policy_decision_making_final.pdf

96   Cf.: http://www.fern.org/sites/fern.org/files/Trading%20away%20rights.pdf

97   Cf.: http://klima-der-gerechtigkeit.boellblog.org/2015/03/12/neues-gesetz-zur-
     nachhaltigen-entwicklung-in-gabun-soll-handel-mit-rechten-lokaler-gemein-
     schaften-ermoeglichen/

98   BBOP stands for "The Business and Biodiversity Offsets Programme" and is a
     co-operation between corporations and financing institutions who wish to test
     and standardise methods for biodiversity offsets.

99   See: http://www.icmm.com/document/4934

100 Cf.: http://www.fauna-flora.org/alive-and-well-for-now-visiting-namibias-ura-
     nium-and-biodiversity-rich-desert/

101 More on this at: http://siansullivan.net/2012/04/24/after-the-green-rush-bio
     diversity-offsets-uranium-power-and-the-calculus-of-casualties-in-greening-
     growth/

102 Over 700 persons and institutions took part in the Commission's public con-
     sultation. Over 40 per cent declared themselves against any kind of offsetting
     and primarily asked for existing regulations to be strengthened instead: http://
     ec.europa.eu/environment/nature/biodiversity/nnl/results_en.htm

103 ETC Group (2009): With Climate Chaos...Who Will Feed Us? The Industrial
     Food Chain/The Peasant Food Web? http://www.etcgroup.org/sites/www.etc
     group.org/files/030913_ETC_WhoWillFeed_AnnotatedPoster_0.pdf

104 Quoted passage translated from the German for convenience. Marcel Hänggi
     (2015): Fortschrittsgeschichten, Frankfurt a. M., p. 29

105 Cf.: http://ec.europa.eu/europe2020/index_de.htm

106 Global Commission on the Economy and Climate (2014): Better Growth, Better
     Climate: The New Climate Economy Report, Chapter 7: Innovation, p. 4

107 Jason Moore: The Capitalocene, Part I, http://www.jasonwmoore.com/uploads/
     The_Capitalocene__Part_I__June_2014.pdf

108 Naturally the so-called Industrial Revolution is much more than an energy revolution. A thorough and readable presentation of the complex processs is found in Jürgen Osterhammel's superb work: The Transformation of the World: A Global History of the Nineteenth Century.

109 See: http://www.ulcos.org/de

110 Cf.: http://www.unep.org/forests/Portals/142/docs/our_vision/Green_Steel.pdf

111 Vaclav Smil (2014): Making the Modern World, Chichester, p. 55

112 Current statistics on worldwide steel production can be found here: http://www.worldsteel.org

113 See: https://www.thyssenkrupp.com/en/nachhaltigkeit/klimaschutz.html

114 Source: https://www.vda.de/en/services/Publications/annual-report-2015.html

115 http://corporateeurope.org/climate-and-energy/2016/01/scandal-hit-car-indus try-driving-seat-new-emissions-regulations

116 The environmental critique of the automobile has almost become a genre. A near "classic" work that is still worth reading is Wolfgang Sachs: "For the Love of the Automobile" – with the nice subtitle: "Looking Back into the History of our Desires". A good update is found in Hänggi 2011.

117 Source: https://www.ipcc.ch/pdf/assessment-report/ar4/wg3/ar4-wg3-chapter5.pdf, p.3

118 See: http://www.dena.de/fileadmin/user_upload/Projekte/Verkehr/Dokumente/Daten-Fakten-Broschuere.pdf (in German)

119 "Trends in CO_2 emissions in the transport sector between 1990 and 2010 varied depending on the form of transport: in the rail and public transport sector and in motorised private transport and inland navigation, CO_2 emissions fell by 37 per cent, 24 per cent, 5 per cent and 1 per cent respectively. Air and road freight registered increases of 82 per cent and 46 per cent in the emission of CO_2", ibid., p. 45 (translated from the German for convenience).

120 https://www.uni-due.de/~hk0378/publikationen/2014/201408_Wirtschafts dienst.pdf (in German)

121 See: http://www.spiegel.de/auto/aktuell/ps-bei-neuwagen-neuer-rekord-in-deutschland-a-1011336.html (in German)

122 Vaclav Smil. loc. cit., p. 133

123 See: http://www.spiegel.de/auto/aktuell/ps-bei-neuwagen-neuer-rekord-in-deutschland-a-1011336.html; www.ace-online.de/nc/der-club/news/jeder-dritte-pkw-in-deutschland-gehoert-einer-frau.html (both in German)

124 See: https://www.lobbycontrol.de/2013/10/autolobby-hat-das-effizienzlabelfuer-autos-selbst-geschrieben/ (in German)

125 A good overview of car manufacturers' lobbying activities in Germany: http://www.faz.net/aktuell/wirtschaft/unternehmen/bmw-daimler-co-die-meister stuecke-der-deutschen-autolobby-12637267.html and http://www.zeit.de/2013/37/autoindustrie-bundesregierung-lobbyismus (both in German)

126 "die flächendeckende Machtergreifung des Autos"; Joachim Radkau (2011): Die Ära der Ökologie, Munich, p. 634

127 Cf.: http://www.ecologic.eu/de/4487

128 Quoted passage translated from the German for convenience. See: http://blog. postwachstum.de/rebound-effekte-vereiteln-eine-hinreichende-entkoppelung-20131021

129 See: http://www.zeit.de/mobilitaet/2014-09/ein-liter-auto-renault

130 Thorough and recent overview of the rebound effect in: Tilman Santarius (2014): Der Rebound-Effekt: ein blinder Fleck der sozial-ökologischen Gesellschafts-transformation, in: GAIA 23/2, pp. 109–117

131 CO_2- or carbon intensity refers to the CO_2 emitted per US dollar of GDP generated, and is used by the Low Carbon Economy Index (LCEI) as a central indicator for the path towards a low-emission economy

132 Tim Jackson (2009): Prosperity without Growth. Economics for a Finite Planet, London

133 http://www.pwc.co.uk/assets/pdf/low-carbon-economy-index-2014.pdf

134 http://www.wired.com/2013/11/vaclav-smil-wired/

135 Tim Jackson, loc. cit., p. 98

136 A good overview is found here: Wuppertal Institut (ed.) (2005): Fair Future. Begrenzte Ressourcen und globale Gerechtigkeit, Munich

137 WWF and Heinrich-Böll-Stiftung (eds.) (2011): How to Feed the World's Growing Billions, https://www.boell.de/sites/default/files/2011-05-How-to-feed-the-Worlds-growing-billions.pdf

138 All figures in this section taken from: http://www.umweltbundesamt.de/themen/klima-energie/erneuerbare-energien/erneuerbare-energien-in-zahlen

139 http://www.unece.org/?id=32790

140 http://www.waldwissen.net/waldwirtschaft/holz/energie/bfw_holz_energie traeger/index_DE

141 Global Commission on the Economy and Climate (2014): Better Growth, Better Climate: The New Climate Economy Report, Chapter Land Use, p. 3

142 http://www.bmel.de/SharedDocs/Downloads/EN/Publications/Understand-ingGlobalFood.pdf?__blob=publicationFile p. 2

143 P. Fitzgerald-Moore, B. J. Parai (1996): The Green Revolution (E-Paper), p. 2, http://people.ucalgary.ca/~pfitzger/green.pdf

144 Marcel Hänggi (2011): Ausgepowert, Zurich, p. 77

145 Norman Uphoff, Emeritus Professor at Cornell University, is one of the most important thought leaders and popular proponents of SRI.

146 http://www.weltagrarbericht.de/leuchttuerme/system-of-rice-intensification. html

147 Both quotes from: http://www.spiegel.de/einestages/kernkraft-damals-abgefah ren-aufs-atom-a-948568.html; quoted passages translated from the German for convenience. The article provides a good overview of early euphoria about nuclear technology. On the same subject: http://www.klimaretter.info/politik/ hintergrund/8916-wie-aus-dem-eis-der-fruehling-werden-sollte. A thorough presentation of the history of the nuclear industry is now available in the factually dense study by Joachim Radkau and Lothar Hahn (2013): Aufstieg und Fall der deutschen Atomwirtschaft, Munich.

148 Can be followed up here: http://library.fes.de/pdf-files/bibliothek/retro-scans/ fa-57721.pdf

149 More in a wonderful article in *hobby* magazine: http://www.castor.de/technik/atomkraft/8_1955/16.html

150 See: http://www.worldenergyoutlook.org/media/weowebsite/2014/141112_WEO_FactSheets.pdf

151 See: http://www.theguardian.com/science/small-world/2013/oct/28/big-nano tech-unexpected-future-apm

152 A thorough and balanced account of nanotechnology is available in: Christian Maier (2014): Nano, Darmstadt

153 A recent overview in: Christoph Then (2015): Handbuch Agro-Gentechnik, Munich. The author talks about "synthetic genetic engineering".

154 ETC Group 2014: The Potential Impacts of Synthetic Biology on Livelihoods and Biodiversity: The Case of Coconut Oil, Palm Kernel Oil and Babassou, http://www.etcgroup.org/sites/www.etcgroup.org/files/Coconut_Potential%20_Impacts_of_SynBio-2.pdf

155 Ibid.

156 http://libcloud.s3.amazonaws.com/93/a2/1/4914/Issue_brief_-_synbio_vanilla.pdf

157 http://www.etcgroup.org/content/case-study-vanilla

158 http://www.etcgroup.org/content/extreme-biotech-meets-extreme-energy

159 http://www.etcgroup.org/content/report-release-outsmarting-nature

160 Although, for the record, by no means all proponents of Green Economy are in favour of geoengineering. Rather, the debate demonstrates that the hope vested in innovation can lead down blind alleys.

161 For further information and background on geoengineering technologies and methods we refer to the ETC Group website (http://www.etcgroup.org/issues/climate-geoengineering) and to the book by Naomi Klein: This Changes Everything.

162 Lydia J. Smith and Margaret S. Tom (2013): "Ecological limits to terrestrial biological carbon dioxide removal", in: Climatic Change, 118 (1), pp. 89–103, http://link.springer.com/article/10.1007%2Fs10584-012-0682-3#page-1

163 http://kevinanderson.info/blog/the-hidden-agenda-how-veiled-techno-utopias-shore-up-the-paris-agreement/

164 Steven Shapin (2007): "What else is new?", in: The New Yorker, 14 May. The article gives a good overview of Edgerton's approach, http://www.newyorker.com/magazine/2007/05/14/what-else-is-new

165 http://www.strategyand.pwc.com/global/home/what-we-think/innovation1000/top-innovators-spenders#/tab-2014

166 Quoted passage translated from the German for convenience. The short text "Steinzeit for ever" ["Stone Age for ever"] is available (in German) here: http://www.mhaenggi.ch/texte/steinzeit-forever

167 More on transformation and alternatives: David Bollier & Silke Helfrich (2012): The Wealth of the Commons – A World Beyond Markets & State (http://www.wealthofthecommons.org/). David Bollier & Silke Helfrich (2015): Patterns of Commoning (http://patternsofcommoning.org/).

168 Naomi Klein (2014): This changes everything, London, p. 201

169 Richard Conniff (2009): "The Political History of Cap and Trade", in: *Smithsonian Magazine*, August, p. 2

170 Ibid. p. 3

171 D. Ellerman et al. (2000): Markets for clean air: the U.S. acid rain program, Cambridge, http://eml.berkeley.edu/~saez/course131/Clean-Air00.pdf, p. 4

172 Global Commission on the Economy and Climate (2014): Better Growth, Better Climate: The New Climate Economy Report, Chapter Innovation, p. 9

173 Ibid., p. 25

174 Two important personalities in recent history have already articulated this basic idea in graphic terms: "The crucial thing is what comes out at the end" (Helmut Kohl 1986); "It doesn't matter what colour a cat is, as long as it catches mice" (Deng Xiaoping).

175 Cf.: http://www.mckinsey.de/sites/mck_files/files/mckinsey_energiewendeindex_et_september_2014.pdf

176 Also designated the "V4", this group is a co-operation between Poland, Hungary, the Czech Republic and Slovakia.

177 Cf. on this the article by Sven Rudolph in: *Ökologisch Wirtschaften*, 2/2014, p. 9, with the symptomatic title: "Ein Hoffnungsschimmer jenseits des Atlantiks" ["A shimmer of hope on the other side of the Atlantic"], http://www.oekologisches-wirtschaften.de/index.php/oew/article/view/1333

178 On this, cf.: https://onclimatechangepolicydotorg.wordpress.com/carbon-pricing/6-energy-taxes-as-carbon-taxes/. What matters, it is argued, is not the exact value at all, but the scale of magnitude.

179 Marcel Hänggi (2011): Ausgepowert, Zürich, p. 261

180 Cf.: http://green.wiwo.de/studie-ab-2020-stagnieren-co2-ausstose-bei-internationalen-flugen/

181 Ibid.

182 See: http://www.iata.org/pressroom/pr/Pages/2013-06-03-05.aspx

183 It is enlightening in this context that the German automobile industry also wants emissions trading: "The German auto industry wants to back the inclusion of motorised road transport within the European emissions trading system. According to information from the newspaper *Welt am Sonntag*, a majority of the vehicle manufacturers organised in the German Association of the Automotive Industry (VDA) back this demand, including heavyweights like BMW and Daimler. With this venture the automotive manufacturers wish to prevent the EU Commission from prescribing ever stricter exhaust standards", http://www.welt.de/wirtschaft/article131974784/Deutsche-Autofahrer-sollen-mehr-fuer-Sprit-zahlen.html

184 CO_2 is not, of course, an ecosystem service provider but its storage in forests counts as an ecosystem service.

185 The quote is taken from a debate with the IMF Managing Director, Christine Lagarde, and the President of the World Bank, Jim Yong Kim, which can be read here: http://www.redd-monitor.org/2013/10/11/climate-change-at-the-world-bank-you-can-imagine-a-future-world-where-carbon-is-really-the-currency-of-the-21st-century/

186 A comprehensive analysis and critique in: Dietz, Engels, Pye, Brunnengräber (eds) (2014): The Political Ecology of Agrofuels, Abingdon

187 Cf. Global Agriculture Report, published in 2008 by the International Assessment of Agricultural Knowledge, Science and Technology for Development (IAASTD). It can be accessed here: http://www.unep.org/dewa/Assessments/Ecosystems/IAASTD/tabid/105853/Default.aspx

188 Pavan Sukhdev (2012): Corporation 2020: Transforming Business for Tomorrow's World. Washington, D.C.

189 Cf. the Rights and Resources Initiative, according to which 24 per cent of forest area in low to medium income countries is said to be in the possession of indigenous peoples and traditional communities, and only 8.7 per cent in the hands of private owners. http://www.rightsandresources.org/publication/protectedareas-and-the-land-rights-of-indigenous-peoples-and-local-communities-current-issues-and-future-agenda/

190 http://www.blickpunkt-lateinamerika.de/news-details/article/rohstoffe-auf-kosten-der-indigenen-bevoelkerung.html?no_cache=1&cHash=8692d7782d0c6763f644b4b43389b219

191 http://mexiko.ahk.de/fileadmin/ahk_mexiko/Inversiones/5_Bergbau_in_Mexiko_CAMEXA_Juni2013.pdf

192 Christa Wichterich, The Future We Want – A Feminist Perspective, Berlin, p. 27 f. http://www.boell.de/sites/default/files/endf_the_future_we_want.pdf

193 A. Biesecker (2011): Vorsorgendes Wirtschaften, in: W. Rätz, T. v. Egan-Krieger et al.: Ausgewachsen, Hamburg, pp. 75–85

194 Jason Moore (2015): Capitalism in the Web of Life

195 More extensive discussion of this issue: Christa Wichterich (2015): Sexual and Reproductive Rights, Berlin (published by the Heinrich-Böll-Stiftung)

196 For an overview of developments in the fair trade sector see http://annualreport.fairtrade.net/en/

197 Cf.: http://power-shift.de/wordpress/wp-content/uploads/2012/06/PowerShift-Saft_fuer_alle_Web_final.pdf

198 Cf.: http://acme-journal.org/index.php/acme/issue/view/73

199 Barbara Unmüßig (2012): Green Sins – How the Green Economy Became a Subject of Controversy, https://www.boell.de/en/ecology/ecology-society-green-economy-social-perspective-15916.html. Laura Hoffmann (2015): Luft als Ware – ein Kampf gegen Windmühlen, http://www.boell.de/de/2015/06/03/luft-als-ware-ein-kampf-gegen-windmuehlen.

200 Colin Crouch: Post-Democracy, Oxford 2004, and Chantal Mouffe (2005): On the Political (Thinking in Action).

201 A current overview of the different approaches for estimating these subsidies: http://ec.europa.eu/economy_finance/publications/economic_briefs/2015/pdf/eb40_en.pdf

202 Quoted from: https://www.boell.de/sites/default/files/redd_in_brazil_2014.pdf

203 The critical groups accuse the RSPO of enabling the further proliferation of palm oil plantations by means of certification instead of protecting the land rights of the local population. On this, cf.: http://wrm.org.uy/articles-from-the-wrm-bulletin/section1/why-the-rspo-facilitates-land-grabs-for-palm-oil/

204 http://www.ohchr.org/EN/HRBodies/HRC/RegularSessions/Session29/Documents/A_HRC_29_25_en.doc

205 https://www.globalwitness.org/en/campaigns/environmental-activists/how-many-more/

206 An insight into the history of the concept: Egon Becker (2013): Die politische Ökologie auf der Suche nach neuen Lebensformen, Institut für sozial-ökologische Forschung, Frankfurt a. M., and in: Markus Wissen (2014): The political ecology of Agrofuels – Conceptual Remarks, in: Kristin Dietz et al. (eds.): The Political Ecology of Agrofuels, The Hague.

207 Quoted passage translated from the German for convenience. Chantal Mouffe (2007): Über das Politische. Wider die kosmopolitische Illusion, Frankfurt a. M., p. 42

208 Ibid., p. 43

209 Gerhard Schick (2014): Machtwirtschaft: Nein Danke! Für eine Wirtschaft, die uns allen dient, Frankfurt a.M.

References

Brand, Ulrich (2012): Schöne Grüne Welt, Berlin

Brand, Ulrich, and Markus Wissen (2013): Imperiale Lebensweise, http://www.buko.info/fileadmin/user_upload/doc/reader/BUKO-Gesnat-Seminar-04-2013-Reader-V1.pdf

Cato, M. S. (2009): Green Economics, London

Conniff, Richard (2009): "The Political History of Cap and Trade", in: *Smithsonian Magazine*, August, http://www.smithsonianmag.com/ist/?next=/air/thepolitical-history-of-cap-and-trade-34711212/

Crouch, Colin (2004): Post-Democracy, Oxford

Dietz, Kristina, et al. (Eds) (2014): The Political Ecology of Agrofuels, Abingdon Eckardt, Felix, and Bettina Hennig (2015): Ökonomische Instrumente und Bewertungen der Biodiversität, Marburg

Ellerman, D., et al. (2000): Markets for clean air: the U.S. acid rain program, Cambridge, http://eml.berkeley.edu/~saez/course131/Clean-Air00.pdf

ETC Group and Heinrich-Böll-Stiftung (2012): Bioma(s)sters Battle to Control the Green Economy, http://us.boell.org/sites/default/files/downloads/Biomassters.pdf

ETC Group (2014): The Potential Impacts of Synthetic Biology on Livelihoods and Biodiversity: The Case of Coconut Oil, Palm Kernel Oil and Babassou, Ottawa

Fatheuer, Thomas (2014): New Economy of Nature, Berlin (published by Heinrich-Böll-Stiftung)

Fitzgerald-Moore, P., and B. J. Parai (1996): The Green Revolution, http://people.ucalgary.ca/~pfitzger/green.pdf

Fücks, Ralf (2015): Green Growth, Smart Growth. A New Approach to Economics, Innovation and the Environment, London/New York (German: Intelligent wachsen. Die grüne Revolution, Munich 2013)

Gleeson-White, Jane (2014): Six Capitals or Can Accounts Save The Planet, New York

Global Commission on the Economy and Climate (2014): Better Growth, Better Climate: The New Climate Economy Report, http://newclimateeconomy.report/

Gottwald, Franz-Theo, and Anita Krätzer (2014): Irrweg Bioökonomie, Frankfurt a. M.

Haas, Jörg (2014): "Die große Wette auf die Selbstzerstörung", in: Politische Ökologie 136, Munich

Hänggi, Marcel (2011): Ausgepowert, Zürich

Hänggi, Marcel (2015): Fortschrittsgeschichten, Frankfurt a. M.

Heinrich-Böll-Stiftung et al. (Eds) (2014): Meat Atlas. Facts and figures about the animals we eat, Berlin

Heinrich-Böll-Stiftung (Ed.) (2014): Resource Politics for a Fair Future. A Memorandum of the Heinrich Böll Foundation, Berlin

Heinrich-Böll-Stiftung et al. (Eds) (2015): Soil Atlas. Facts and figures about earth, land and fields, Berlin

Heinrich-Böll-Stiftung and BUND (Eds) (2015): Coal Atlas. Facts and figures on a fossil fuel, Berlin

Helfrich, Silke, and Heinrich-Böll-Stiftung (Eds) (2012): Commons – Für eine neue Politik jenseits von Markt und Staat, Bielefeld

Helfrich, Silke, Bollier, D., and Heinrich-Böll-Stiftung (Eds) (2015): Die Welt der Commons. Muster gemeinsamen Handelns, Bielefeld

Hoffmann, Ulrich (2015): Can Green Growth Really Work, Berlin, https://www.boell. de/sites/default/files/e-paper_hoffmann_green_growth_1.pdf

IAASTD (2009): International Assessment of Agricultural Knowledge Science and Technology for Development, Agriculture at Crossroads, Global Report, Washington, D.C.

IPCC (2007): Mitigation of Climate Change. Contribution of Working Group III to the Fifth Assessment Report of the Intergovernmental Panel on Climate Change

IPCC (2014): Summary for Policymakers, in: Climate Change 2014: Impacts, Adaptation, and Vulnerability

Jackson, Tim (2009): Wohlstand ohne Wachstum, Munich (published by Heinrich-Böll-Stiftung)

Jacobs, Martin (2012): Green Growth: Economic Theory and Political Discourse. Grantham Research Institute on Climate Change and the Environment, Working Paper 92

Kill, Jutta (2014): Economic Valuation of Nature, Brussels, http://www.rosalux.de/ fileadmin/rls_uploads/pdfs/sonst_publikationen/Economic-Valuation-of-Nature. pdf

Kill, Jutta (2015): REDD: A Collection of Conflicts, Contradictions and Lies, Montevideo, http://wrm.org.uy/wp-content/uploads/2014/12/REDD-A-Collection-of-Conflict_Contradictions_Lies_expanded.pdf

Klein, Naomi (2014): This changes everything, London

Kössler, Georg (2012): Geo-Engineering: Gibt es wirklich einen Plan(eten) B? Berlin, https://www.boell.de/sites/default/files/GeoEngineering_V02_kommentierbar. pdf

Moreno, Camila, Daniel Speich Chassé and Lili Fuhr (2015): Carbon Metrics – Global abstractions and ecological epistemicide, Berlin (published by Heinrich-Böll-Stiftung), https://www.boell.de/en/2015/11/09/carbon-metrics

Maier, Christian (2014): Nano, Darmstadt

Moore, Jason W. (2015): Capitalism in the Web of Life: Ecology and the Accumulation of Capital, London/New York

Mouffe, Chantal (2005): On the Political (Thinking in Action), London (German: Über das Politische – Wider die kosmopolitische Illusion, Frankfurt a. M. 2007)

Naturkapital Deutschland – TEEB DE (2012): Der Wert der Natur für Wirtschaft und Gesellschaft, Leipzig and Bonn

Osterhammel, Jürgen (2009): Die Verwandlung der Welt, Munich

Pretty, J., et al. (2006): "Resource-conserving agriculture increases yields in developing countries", in: *Environmental Science & Technology* 3(1), 24–43

Radkau, Joachim (2011): Die Ära der Ökologie, Munich

Radkau, Joachim, and Lothar Hahn (2013): Aufstieg und Fall der deutschen Atomwirtschaft, Munich

Rights and Resources Initiative (2015): Protected Areas and the Land Rights of
Indigenous Peoples and Local Communities, www.rightsandresources.org/pub-
lication/protected-areas-and-the-land-rights-of-indigenous-peoples-and-local-
communities-current-issues-and-future-agenda/

Sachs, Wolfgang (1991): Die Liebe zum Automobil, Reinbek

Sachs, Wolfgang, and Tilman Santarius (2014): Rethink statt Rebound: Der Effizienz-
revolution muss eine Suffizienzrevolution vorangehen, in: *Factory*, No. 3

Santarius, Tilman (2014): Der Rebound-Effekt: ein blinder Fleck der sozial-ökologischen Gesellschaftstransformation, in: *GAIA* 23 (2)

Schick, Gerhard (2014): Machtwirtschaft – Nein Danke! Frankfurt a. M./New York

Schildberg, Cäcilie (2014): A Caring and Sustainable Economy, Berlin, http://library.
fes.de/pdf-files/iez/10809.pdf

Schneidewind, Uwe, and Angelika Zahrnt (2013): Damit gutes Leben einfacher wird.
Perspektiven einer Suffizienzpolitik, Munich

Shrivastava, Aseem, and Ashish Kothari (2012): Churning The Earth – The Making
of Global India, London

Smil, Vaclav (2014): Making the Modern World, Chichester

Sukhdev, Pavan (2012): Corporation 2020: Transforming Business for Tomorrow's
World. Washington D.C.

Then, Christoph (2015): Handbuch Agro-Gentechnik, Munich

Umweltbundesamt (2013): Globale Landflächen und Biomasse – nachhaltig und res-
sourcenschonend nutzen, Dessau

UNEP (2011): Towards a Green Economy: Pathways to Sustainable Development and
Poverty Eradication, p. 16, www.unep.org/greeneconomy

Unmüßig, Barbara, Wolfgang Sachs and Thomas Fatheuer (2012): Critique of the
Green Economy – Toward Social and Environmental Equity, Berlin (published
by Heinrich-Böll-Stiftung), https://www.boell.de/de/node/278965

Unmüßig, Barbara (2014): Monetizing Nature – Taking Precaution on a Slippery Slope,
https://us.boell.org/2014/08/26/monetizing-nature-taking-precaution-slippery
slope Welzer, Harald, Dana Giesecke and Luise Tremel (Eds) (2014): Futur Zwei,
Zukunftsalmanach 2015/2016, Frankfurt a. M.

Wichterich, Christa (2012): Die Zukunft, die wir wollen, Berlin (published by
Heinrich-Böll-Stiftung), http://www.boell.de/sites/default/files/Feministische_
Zukunft-i.pdf

Wichterich, Christa (2015): Sexuelle und reproduktive Rechte, Berlin (published by
Heinrich-Böll-Stiftung), http://www.boell.de/de/2015/09/18/sexuelle-und-repro
duktive-rechte

World Bank (2012): Inclusive Green Growth, Washington, D.C., http://siteresources.
worldbank.org/EXTSDNET/Resources/Inclusive_Green_Growth_May_2012.
pdf

World Bank (2014): State and Trends of Carbon Pricing, Washington, D.C., http://www-wds.worldbank.org/external/default/WDSContentServer/WDSP/IB/2014/05/27/000456286_20140527095323/Rendered/PDF/882840AR0REPLA00EPI2102680Box385232.pdf

Wuppertal Institut (Ed.) (2005): Fair Future. Begrenzte Ressourcen und globale Gerechtigkeit, Munich

WWF and Heinrich-Böll-Stiftung (Eds) (2011): How to Feed the World's Growing Billions, https://www.boell.de/sites/default/files/2011-05-How-to-feed-the-Worlds-growing-billions.pdf

About the authors

Thomas Fatheuer

is a social scientist and lived in Brazil from 1992 to 2010, most recently as head of the Heinrich Böll Foundation's office in Rio de Janeiro. Prior to that he worked on forest conservation projects in the Amazon region for the German Development Service (DED) and German Technical Cooperation (GTZ). Currently, he is living and working as an author and consultant in Berlin. He is the author of numerous publications on the Brazilian development model, the conservation of tropical forests and the concept of *Buen Vivir*.

Lili Fuhr

is a graduate geographer and, since 2008, heads the international Ecology and Sustainable Development Department at the Heinrich Böll Foundation with a special focus on international climate and resource politics. She blogs regularly at www.klima-der-gerechtigkeit.de.

Barbara Unmüßig

is a political scientist and, since 2002, Co-President of the Heinrich Böll Foundation. She has acted since 2009 as deputy member of the Board of Trustees of the German Institute for Human Rights (DIMR). Her work focuses on issues such as the social aspects of globalisation, human and women's rights and international climate, resource and agricultural policy. Among other roles, she is chair of the jury for the Anne Klein Women's Award, which has been presented annually since 2012 by the Heinrich Böll Foundation. Barbara Unmüßig has published numerous articles for books and journals.